Virtue in an Age of Identity Politics

Virtue in an Age of Identity Politics

A Stoic Approach to Social Justice

Jonathan D. Church

ROWMAN & LITTLEFIELD
Lanham • Boulder • New York • London

Published by Rowman & Littlefield
An imprint of The Rowman & Littlefield Publishing Group, Inc.
4501 Forbes Boulevard, Suite 200, Lanham, Maryland 20706
www.rowman.com
86-90 Paul Street, London EC2A 4NE, United Kingdom

British Library Cataloguing in Publication Information Available

Library of Congress Cataloging-in-Publication Data
Names: Church, Jonathan D., 1978– author.
Title: Virtue in an age of identity politics : a stoic approach to social
    justice / Jonathan D. Church.
Description: Lanham : Rowman & Littlefield, [2022] | Includes
    bibliographical references and index. | Summary: "Virtue in an Age of
    Identity Politics examines current social justice activism through the
    lens of Stoic philosophy. While developing a critique of Critical Social
    Justice, it also explains how Stoicism overlaps with Critical Social
    Justice in the interest of healing social divisions and promoting honest
    and nuanced conversations about justice."—Provided by publisher.
Identifiers: LCCN 2021055269 (print) | LCCN 2021055270 (ebook) | ISBN
    9781475863147 (cloth) | ISBN 9781475863154 (paperback) | ISBN
    9781475863161 (epub)
Subjects: LCSH: Social justice. | Identity politics. | Stoics.
Classification: LCC HM671 .C58 2022 (print) | LCC HM671 (ebook) | DDC
    303.3/72—dc23/eng/20220204
LC record available at https://lccn.loc.gov/2021055269
LC ebook record available at https://lccn.loc.gov/2021055270

*Dedicated to David Randall Church, Linda Carroll Church,
Kara Simmons, and Lincoln Lee Simmons-Church*

"It is according to opinion that we suffer. A man is as bad as he has convinced himself that he is."—Seneca, *Letters from a Stoic*, #78

Contents

Contents

Acknowledgments

I begin by expressing sincere gratitude to Kai Whiting, who provided me with invaluable insight and many helpful resources on the philosophy of Stoicism. His review of earlier drafts of the manuscript resulted in a much stronger final manuscript than would have otherwise been realized. His contribution to this work proved a genuine display of Stoic virtue in being straightforward with his constructive criticism while providing guidance on how to improve the analysis.

Next, I would like to thank Sam Hoadley-Brills, whose excellent review helped sharpened my analysis of critical theory and my discussions of Kant, critical race theory, and other aspects of modern philosophy. Donald Weise deserves my sincere thanks for his thorough review of the manuscript. Likewise, David Maynard, Justin Yarros, and Rick Heller reviewed drafts and provided valuable comments, edits, and corrections that improved the final manuscript.

I am grateful to Wilhelm Cortez, who gave me the opportunity to publish several articles on social justice at the Good Men Project when I began thinking about the controversies in social justice activism that emerged in the 2010s. I would also like to thank Claire Lehmann and Jamie Palmer of *Quillette* for publishing two essays that were adapted to two sections in this book.

Finally, I am indebted to Curtis Bowman, who taught many of the philosophy courses I took as an undergraduate student at the University of Pennsylvania. Dr. Bowman played a crucial role in helping me understand the ideas that underlie "continental" philosophy and that have become relevant to controversies surrounding "social justice" scholarship and activism in the first decades of this century.

Introduction

In my previous book, *Reinventing Racism: Why "White Fragility" Is the Wrong Way to Think about Racial Inequality*, I presented a rebuttal to the thesis proposed by author and activist Dr. Robin DiAngelo that "white fragility" explains why it is so hard to talk to white people about racism. DiAngelo defines white fragility as "a state in which even a minimum amount of racial stress becomes intolerable, triggering a range of defensive moves" that "include the outward display of emotions such as anger, fear, and guilt, and behaviors such as argumentation, silence, and leaving the stress-inducing situation," all of which "function to reinstate white racial equilibrium."

"Racial stress," she claims, "results from an interruption to what is racially familiar," such as "suggesting that a white person's viewpoint comes from a racialized frame of reference," which apparently challenges "objectivity," and "suggesting that group membership is significant," which purportedly challenges "individualism."[1] DiAngelo posited white fragility as an impediment to discussions with white people about racism in her 2004 PhD dissertation.[2] The idea eventually morphed into her 2018 book, *White Fragility: Why It's So Hard to Talk to White People about Racism*,[3] which topped the bestseller lists during racial unrest in America in 2020.

In *Reinventing Racism*, I argued that "white fragility" is, in practice, a rhetorical trap that prevents constructive dialogue on issues related to race. By interpreting every objection to her claims about racism as a psychological defense mechanism that reflects ignorance on the part of white people, she effectively assumes "guilt" with every assertion of "innocence." I also argued that her theory relies on the dubious premise of implicit bias; relies on a faulty way of understanding racism; has serious methodological problems; exploits narratives at the expense of facts; distorts the Enlightenment and the Frankfurt School's conception of Critical Theory; runs afoul of reason and logic; replaces scholarship with sermonizing; is a rhetorical weapon for activist bullies; and imposes a substantial "transaction cost" that impedes the pursuit of racial justice.

In taking aim specifically at the theory of white fragility, I was also taking aim more generally at the broader paradigm of "Critical Social Justice" that informs white fragility theory. As I explain in more detail in chapters 1 and 2 of this book, Critical Theory is a method of inquiry that examines the historical and ideological circumstances that underlie conditions of societal stratification and subordination. It has its roots in the continental Western philosophical tradition and drives much of the intellectual vision and agenda of twenty-first-century social justice activism.

DiAngelo, author of a book on social justice education, embraces Critical Theory as a key intellectual framework for thinking about white fragility and social justice. Given the roots of contemporary social justice activism in Critical Theory, DiAngelo and her colleague Özlem Sensoy describe the framework for the modern social justice movement as "Critical Social Justice"[4] (DiAngelo and Sensoy use lowercase letters, but I capitalize to highlight the distinct framework).

In sum, my book was designed as a critique. Critique only goes so far, however, and I have often been asked: what is the alternative? In the final chapter of *Reinventing Racism*, I proposed an alternative framed in terms of *economic* theory, describing whiteness as a form of property that historically turned public goods, such as basic rights that everyone should enjoy in society, into club goods historically enjoyed only by white people. For example, the right to expect fair treatment from the police is a "good privilege" that should not be "checked" but expanded to everyone—i.e., it should be a "public good" for everyone rather than a "club good" for white people only.

In this book, I adopt a different approach that directly confronts the *philosophical* framework of Critical Social Justice in which white fragility theory and modern social justice activism are steeped. This philosophical approach is chosen specifically to help navigate the contentious discourse on power and privilege that dominates the Critical Social Justice paradigm to which DiAngelo is committed.

This is a discourse whose lexicon includes terms and phrases like trigger warnings, microaggressions, safe spaces, intersectionality, toxic masculinity, and whiteness, all of which I address in this book. This lexicon is integral to a conception of social justice that, focused on social hierarchies, aims to minimize the adverse *impact* of behaviors and institutions on people based on their racial, gender, or other social identity. Impact is measured in terms of psychological and emotional harm, social and economic inequality, and overall well-being.

The specific approach I adopt draws from the ancient Greek and Roman philosophy of Stoicism. It may be jarring to readers unfamiliar with the (upper-case) Stoicism of ancient philosophers, and more familiar with the (lower-case) stoicism of contemporary understanding, to think that being

"Stoic" has anything to offer while the world seems to be crumbling under the weight of injustice. Indeed, our layman understanding of being "stoic" may sound like the last thing we need in a quest for social justice that would seem to be more in the domain of freedom fighters and utopian idealists.

It is my hope this book can disabuse skeptics. Stoicism as it was conceived by ancient Greek and Roman philosophers is quite different from lay conceptions of "stoic" persons who are noticeably detached, unemotional, and apparently resigned to their fates. Stoicism is not a philosophy of complacency. Nor is it about simply "bucking up" in the face of adversity. It is, in fact, a philosophy of action that can yield enormous benefits, not only in terms of social outcomes, but also personal well-being. It is also worth pointing out, though I don't explore this point in this book, that Stoicism has much in common with eastern philosophies such as Buddhism and Taoism.

Strictly speaking, Stoicism is about the pursuit of *eudaimonia*, a life of well-being or flourishing that stems from the cultivation of virtue. The Stoics had a specific conception of virtue that I will attempt to explain, starting in chapter 1, but more thoroughly in chapter 3. In brief, the Stoics espouse four interconnected, cardinal virtues: wisdom, temperance, courage, and justice.

These four virtues were widely admired in the ancient world and were derived from Plato, who expounded on them in *The Republic*. On the basis of these virtues, as well as various contributions to our understanding of human nature and the natural world, the Stoics developed an ethical framework that lands fundamentally on the vital importance of reason, social obligations, and the inherent capability of all human beings to live well together under all circumstances.

In this book, I also want to suggest that, as a philosophy anchored on virtue as the foundation of thought and action, Stoicism emphasizes the moral *intent* of human beings who make up a social community. As such, Stoicism shares a fundamental concern of social justice activism with making the world a better place. It is also aligned with Critical Social Justice in being concerned with how each of us can contribute to the collective effort to minimize the adverse impact of institutional injustice on people based on their racial, gender, or other social identity.

Unlike the contemporary social justice movement, however, Stoicism is less inclined to see power and privilege as the most crucial impediments to a well-lived life. It is also more inclined to treat other human beings as members of a common humanity than as members of social groups. That is not to say that it ignores power and privilege as irrelevant to human flourishing and social progress, nor does it entail neglecting the social implications of group identity.

It is to say instead that prioritizing virtue, as understood by the Stoics, rather than identity politics (which is political activism on behalf of marginalized social identities and that leans heavily on a discourse of power and privilege), is key to human flourishing and social progress. For the Stoics, power and privilege are "indifferents"—aspects of the world around us that are important in terms of whether we use them virtuously, but not fundamental to well-being in themselves.

Perhaps the most salient way identity politics comes up short is that it gives rise to a culture of victimhood that emphasizes the impact, rather than the intent, of thoughts and actions. From "safe spaces" to "trigger warnings" to "microaggressions," there is an insistence that well-being depends crucially on the sensitivity of other people rather than on tending to our internal capacity to cultivate our own character.

This is not to ignore that people can be insensitive or that what they say and do can have hurtful impacts on other people. But there is something different about modern social justice activism. Power and privilege are central themes in a moral and political outlook concerned with *the circumstances which constrain our choices and actions rather than on the choices we make and the actions we undertake in response to these circumstances.*

For now, the point I want to convey is that we control only our intent, but we do not control all the external factors that determine the impact of our actions. This point is key for an understanding of the Stoic conception of virtue as the foundation of a well-lived life. The ancient Stoics did not talk in terms of intent and impact in the same way as people involved in the contemporary discourse about social justice activism. For the Stoics, intent was a matter of actively developing one's character so that it is virtuous. But Stoicism can help us think about the relative importance of intent and impact in analyzing issues that galvanize concerns about social justice in today's world.

As the author of Intelligent Virtue, Julia Annas, writes, the virtuous life is found in the living of a life, not its circumstances:

> The circumstances of your life are the factors whose existence in your life are not under your control. You are a particular age, with a particular genetic disposition, gender, height, etc.; you have a particular nationality, culture, and language, have received a particular upbringing and education, have a particular family, employment, and so on. It's not that you can't do anything about these factors, but it's not up to you that they are there in your life. . . . The living of your life is the way you deal with the circumstances of your life.[5]

The living of your life takes priority because it is the living of your life, not the circumstances handed to you by fate or fortune, that you control. This distinction provides us with a core life lesson of Stoicism: the dichotomy of control. It is not simply that we control how we live but not the circumstances handed to us. In prioritizing the pursuit of virtue, Stoicism promotes the cultivation of good character as the path to *eudaimonia*. This pursuit is a unique function of being human because it is rational, relying on the exercise of reason, given to us by nature. Since reason and virtue depend wholly on us, we have autonomy in the rational pursuit of virtue.

In autonomy, we find contentment. From a Stoic perspective, if the impact of our actions does not work out the way we intended, we can learn to accept the outcome as being beyond our control, if only because we cannot change the past, while recognizing an opportunity to respond to new circumstances. It is always up to us to determine how to exercise our moral intent, while accepting that there are things outside our control that may determine the impact of our actions in ways we did not intend.

If things do not work out as planned or expected, we can identify new opportunities to respond virtuously. Reason guides us to virtue, and virtue is about living rightly. The well-lived life, i.e., *eudaimonia*, arises in large part from a commitment to responding to circumstances in accord with virtue, i.e., with wisdom, courage, temperance, and justice. In other words, it's about living rightly—or to borrow the title from an excellent book about Stoicism, it's about *being better*.[6]

The Stoic perspective helps us to see the advantages of focusing on intent rather than impact. But this does not imply that Stoics do not care about impact, as if the purpose of Stoicism is to look inward without regard for the world around us. As Professor Gregory Sadler, a noted expert on Stoicism, explains, Stoicism is a self-centered philosophy, but not "in the way that most people use that term."[7] For example, the notion that egoism and altruism are mutually exclusive is a false dichotomy. Instead, we have obligations to ourselves as rational creatures concerned with our self-preservation and our own flourishing as human beings, but as our rational capacity matures, we naturally widen our scope to take more people into account in our thoughts and actions.

This clarification highlights a key Stoic tenet that we are social creatures, connected with one another as part of the natural world and as part of society, and depending on each other for our well-being. A central goal of this book is to lay out a Stoic approach to social justice that not only differs, but also overlaps, with prevailing ideas and sentiments about how activists can work on behalf of social justice. The crucial importance that Stoic philosophy places on the obligations our rational nature imposes on us as social creatures is an example of how Stoicism and Critical Social Justice overlap.

This overlap is best illustrated by clearing up a common misconception that Stoicism is about complacency. As noted, the Stoic focus on developing a virtuous character leads us to the dichotomy of control, a core tenet of Stoicism explored throughout this book. The idea is that we should be concerned only with things under our control. By cultivating wisdom, one of the four cardinal virtues that the Stoics embraced, we can learn to distinguish between the things under our control and things not under our control. Then we can act accordingly (with courage, temperance, and an eye toward justice).

The dichotomy of control is nicely captured by the famous "serenity prayer": "God grant me the serenity to accept the things I cannot change, courage to change the things I can, and the wisdom to know the difference." But this is not about resigning ourselves to our fate. It is instead about understanding our circumstances, and the constraints they entail, to figure out how to enact virtue as best we can.

This outlook serves two purposes. First, it helps alleviate anxieties and worries about things that happen that are not our fault. Second, it redirects attention to the things we can control, in effect empowering us to discover all the ways in which we *can* change the circumstances in which we live. It's about living virtuously in our realm of autonomy, not about being slaves to our circumstances. Not *worrying* about things not under our control does not mean *ignoring* things outside our control.

Let us consider an example.

On April 20, 2021, former Minneapolis police officer Derek Chauvin became the first white police officer in Minnesota to be convicted of murdering a black civilian. George Floyd died when Chauvin knelt on the neck of the handcuffed Floyd for over nine minutes on May 25, 2020. Upon news of the conviction, roars of approval erupted from crowds outside the courthouse. However, many commentators were quick to say that the verdict was not about justice, but accountability. For example, NBA basketball superstar LeBron James tweeted the single word in capital letters: "ACCOUNTABILITY." The conviction of Mr. Chauvin was welcomed, but in the view of many activists and commentators, there was much work yet to be done to achieve racial justice.

After the conviction, Minnesota governor Tim Walz thanked Darnella Frazier, the young woman who captured the scene on her phone. As Mr. Chauvin bent his knee on Mr. Floyd's neck, surrounded by three other police officers, Ms. Frazier and other bystanders likely felt powerless to prevent the suffering of Mr. Floyd. In this sense, the event was out of their control. Ms. Frazier, however, had the presence of mind to film the encounter. "Taking that video," Mr. Walz said, "I think many folks know, is maybe the only reason that Derek Chauvin will go to prison."[8]

Given the uncertainties of legal proceedings, and two autopsy reports that differed on key details, the implication seemed to be that Chauvin had a good chance of escaping conviction absent the convincing evidence of Ms. Frazier's video. Why? Because it was four white cops against one black civilian. Even though a black civilian was dead, the "system" was set up to protect white police officers (who were seen not as individuals who could have acted more virtuously, but as representatives of the system). In other words, the circumstances in which Mr. Floyd found himself had more power over his fate than any choice or action he could have undertaken in response to these circumstances.

The same goes for the bystanders such as Ms. Frazier, as well as the prosecutors, commentators, activists, and many others who subsequently sought to hold Mr. Chauvin accountable in court after he killed Mr. Floyd. Undoubtedly, there is merit to the belief that prosecutors would have faced a steep uphill battle in their attempt to convict Mr. Chauvin without video evidence. Conviction is never certain given the presumption of innocence and the vagaries of legal proceedings. Moreover, no white police officer in Minnesota had ever been convicted of murdering a black civilian, which presumably sheds light on institutional rigidities in the courts and in law enforcement that militate against the smooth and successful administration of justice.

Indeed, as America grappled with racial unrest in the wake of Mr. Floyd's murder, many were quick to highlight, or dispute, the data on systemic racism in police shootings. Given the backdrop of historical disparities in how black civilians are treated by the police, people were not without good reason to believe that Mr. Floyd never stood a chance. This is the key point that lies behind the distinction between justice and accountability. For once, we saw accountability in a system that all too often fails black Americans. Justice is not about one conviction, but about constructing a system in which convictions of guilty parties are a matter of course.

The social unrest experienced in American cities in 2020, then, is clearly understandable, and if this is what people mean when they talk about fighting for social justice, it certainly sounds perverse to say that social justice activism has become controversial. Social justice, after all, is a goal to which, in principle, all of us should aspire. The controversy, however, is not about challenging a status quo that perpetuates injustice, but about the broader set of policies, ideas, and practices that contemporary activists advocate as the "right" way to address social injustice. In other words, people disagree on what we need to do to make the world a better place.

These disagreements have become so visceral and contentious, in an era in which social media and YouTube serve as venues on which controversial opinions can go viral with unprecedented rapidity, that serious concerns have emerged about instantaneous campaigns by social media "mobs" and custodians of political factions on the Left and Right to banish heterodox "undesirables" from society, either because they allegedly signal reactionary opposition to social justice, or because their progressive advocacy of social justice takes on a Manichean, almost messianic, fervor that turns political correctness into what many perceive as a McCarthyite witch hunt. One might say we need a healthy way to think about social justice in an age of identity politics.

Ms. Frazier provides us with an example of the Stoic approach I advocate in this book. She had the presence of mind to film the deadly encounter and the courage to offer it up to the authorities in the interest of holding the officers accountable. As a result, despite being unable to keep Mr. Floyd alive, she contributed to the overall effort to bring justice to the "system." I call this a Stoic approach because it is focuses on the extent to which our own character is virtuous, which involves discovering the unique ways in which each of us can contribute to a better world. Ms. Frazier found herself in a position to advance the cause of justice. She did so wisely. She also did so courageously.

Stoicism, as developed by Greek and Roman Stoic philosophers over a five-hundred-year period in the ancient world, is the healthy perspective we need, in lieu of, or at least as a supplement to, the Critical Social Justice paradigm that currently dominates progressive discourse. This book attempts to explain this philosophical alternative to Critical Social Justice. The ancient Greek and Roman philosophy of Stoicism provides a viable and helpful philosophical framework, rooted in virtue ethics, which prioritizes moral intent *without* neglecting moral impact.

OUTLINE OF THE BOOK

This book is the outgrowth of a decades-long personal preoccupation with the nature of justice. This preoccupation stems not from my choice of profession, but from a deeply felt interest in questions of a philosophical nature that took root in high school. These questions continued with me throughout my college years, my maturation as an adult, and my professional career as an economist. This preoccupation provides the backdrop from which chapter 1 introduces Stoicism and Critical Social Justice by showing the ways they overlap and the ways they contrast with each other, allowing us to see possibilities for a synergistic connection between the individualistic cultivation of a virtuous character and the collective pursuit of a more just society.

This book deals specifically with social justice as it is framed and understood by scholars and activists who are involved or otherwise interested in social justice movements in the twenty-first century. This scholarship and activism are heavily anchored on Critical Theory, a philosophical framework I studied as an undergraduate philosophy major at the University of Pennsylvania. Chapter 2 provides an in-depth look at the historical development of Critical Social Justice, what it means, and what its strengths and weaknesses are in relation to what a Stoic perspective has to offer.

In recent years, I have been studying Stoicism as a practical philosophy that I have found helpful for thinking about several challenges I have confronted in my life. In doing so, Stoicism has increasingly struck me as a viable alternative to Critical Social Justice for thinking about the challenges that society faces in the quest for social justice. In chapter 3, I explore and explain the ancient philosophy of Greco-Roman Stoicism as a viable alternative to Critical Social Justice.

Turning to applications, chapter 4 analyzes critical whiteness studies, an increasingly influential aspect of Critical Social Justice and the underlying framework for white fragility theory, from a Stoic perspective. Chapter 4 also examines the hit show *Breaking Bad* as a case study in how Stoicism can help us think fruitfully about critical whiteness studies in particular and Critical Social Justice in general. The final chapter examines former United States president Abraham Lincoln as a Stoic model of leadership for the social justice movement. I conclude the book with an overview of how Stoicism can help us think about social justice in the wake of the challenging year of 2020.

NOTES

1. Robin DiAngelo, "White Fragility," *International Journal of Critical Pedagogy,* Vol. 3 (3) (2011), p. 57.

2. Robin DiAngelo, "Whiteness in Racial Dialogue: A Discourse Analysis," PhD dissertation, University of Washington, 2004.

3. Robin DiAngelo, *White Fragility: Why It's So Hard for White People to Talk about Racism* (Boston, MA: Beacon Press, 2018).

4. Özlem Sensoy and Robin DiAngelo, *Is Everyone Really Equal? An Introduction to Key Concepts in Social Justice Education* (New York: Teachers College Press, 2012), p. xviii.

5. Julia Annas, *Intelligent Virtue* (Oxford: Oxford University Press, 2011), pp. 92–93.

6. Kai Whiting and Leonidas Konstantakos, *Being Better: Stoicism for a World Worth Living in* (Novato, CA: New World Library, 2021).

7. Is the Philosophy of Stoicism Self-Centered? Answers to Common Questions (0:30): https://www.youtube.com/watch?v=nuit5Kf5BH8

8. Holly Yan, "A Teen with 'a Cell Phone and Sheer Guts' Is Credited for Derek Chauvin's Murder Conviction," CNN, April 21, 2012.

Chapter 1

Why a Stoic Approach
to Social Justice?

In the second half of the fourth century BC, the age of Alexander the Great, a man named Zeno of Citium was sailing along the Mediterranean Sea when he suffered a shipwreck and washed up at the Greek port of Piraeus, not far from the city of Athens. The shipwreck sank all hopes of any fortune he might earn from selling the luxurious purple dye he had had aboard.

Accounts vary about whether Zeno was a penniless immigrant or had preexisting investments as he made his way to Athens. But whatever the case, he soon found himself in a bookstore in Athens listening to the bookseller, who was reading passages from Xenophon's *Memorabilia*. This work consisted of Xenophon's recollections of Socratic conversations about philosophy.

Having previously been given advice by the Delphic oracle (whose cryptic remarks on fate were taken seriously by the ancient Greeks) that "to live the best life . . . he should have intercourse with the dead,"[1] Zeno was so captivated by what this dead philosopher named Socrates was saying in the *Memorabilia* that he immediately asked the bookseller where he could find someone like Socrates.

As fate would have it, the Cynic philosopher Crates was strolling past the bookstore. The bookseller pointed to Crates. "Follow him." Zeno did, came under the tutelage of Crates, and eventually went on to found a school of philosophy known as Stoicism, named after the *stoa poikile*, or "painted porch," in which Stoic philosophers and students gathered publicly to discuss ideas.

Focused on virtue ethics while synthesizing aspects of various ancient schools like Cynicism and Platonism, Stoicism would become one of the dominant philosophical systems in the Greek and Roman world for the next five centuries. Insisting that virtue, which can be described as excellence of character, is all you need to be happy (what the Stoic philosophers called *eudaimonia*), the Stoics were inspired by the Socratic love of wisdom and the notion that the unexamined life is not worth living. But wisdom was not about knowledge for knowledge's sake.

For the Stoics, the ideal life is one in which reason ensures that one's thoughts and actions are anchored on four cardinal virtues and that they bring one into harmony with nature, which the Stoics conceived as a structured order in a universe (more succinctly called Logos) that is rational in the sense that it is intelligible to us. These virtues are wisdom, courage, moderation, and justice, described by Stoic author and philosopher Massimo Pigliucci as follows:

> Practical wisdom is the knowledge of what experiences or actions are truly good or bad (as distinct from what others may say counts as good or bad), particularly in regard to how they affect one's own character. Courage means the willingness to do what we think is right, regardless of its potentially negative consequences for ourselves. Justice means acting fairly towards others—behaving towards them as we would like them to behave toward us. And temperance is the notion that we should do things in right measure, neither too much nor too little.[2]

These virtues are their own reward. "The reward for all the virtues," wrote the ancient Roman Senator and Stoic philosopher Seneca the Younger in *Letters from a Stoic,* "lies in the virtues themselves. Because they are not practicing with a view to recompense; the wage of a good deed is to have done it" Letter 81).

We will explore these Stoic virtues in more detail throughout the book as we develop the theme that Stoicism provides a viable alternative to Critical Social Justice as a philosophical framework for thinking about the quest for social justice. But let's begin by acknowledging that it may seem too idealistic to claim that these basic virtues are sufficient for a life of lasting happiness. We also might be skeptical that the Stoic cultivation of character provides a good foundation for the pursuit of social justice in a world in which structural inequalities appear to be pervasive and deeply entrenched.

If, however, we consider the ancient philosopher Socrates who inspired Zeno, we get a glimpse of how virtue can carve a path toward both lasting happiness and lasting commitment to social justice.

One key observation is that Socrates was like many ancient philosophers in being concerned above all with how to live a good life. As Pierre Hadot notes in *The Inner Citadel*, "a philosopher in antiquity was not someone who wrote philosophical books, but someone who led a philosophical life."[3] The concern with virtue was not simply an academic matter of fine-tuning our abstract understanding of justice, or more generally of what virtue entails, but learning how to employ virtue in our lives to make us better people, not only for ourselves but for other people as well.

Right away, then, we perceive a synergistic connection between the individualistic concern with cultivation of character and the collective concern with making the world a better place. These individualistic and collective concerns are both Stoic concerns. The goal of this chapter is to introduce Stoicism and Critical Social Justice by providing a preliminary look at how they compare, and contrast, with each other, allowing us to see possibilities for synergy between the individualistic cultivation of a virtuous character and the collective pursuit of a more just society.

We can get a brief glimpse by considering Plato's *The Apology*, in which Socrates defends himself against charges of impiety and corrupting the youth of ancient Athens, and *The Crito*, in which Socrates explained why it was the right thing to do to drink the hemlock rather than escape from prison. First, one can observe the courage with which Socrates faced trial and death, buoyed by his commitment to a life of philosophical inquiry and the intellectual wherewithal to sustain it. Second, one can observe that Socrates never wavered in doing what he thought was right.

Certainly, from our modern perch, separated by over two thousand years from the courtroom in which Socrates was persecuted, it can be hard to fathom the gravity of what Socrates was up against and the poise with which he confronted it, claiming with his characteristic equanimity that his accusers could never harm him. But Socrates was quite serious in doing what he thought was right—first, spreading the message that wisdom consists of the recognition of one's ignorance; second, insisting in all sincerity that he was providing a moral service to the city-state of Athens by asking questions designed to test the wisdom of the supposed illuminati of Athenian society.

For these and other reasons, Socrates was sentenced to death. Socrates refused an offer to have the charges dropped if he would cease to practice philosophy. He also refused an offer from friends to help him escape prison. In both cases, it was a matter of virtue. To cease to practice philosophy would be to give up on the pursuit of wisdom (one of the four cardinal virtues). That he simply could not do. To disobey the laws would be to undermine justice (another cardinal virtue), which he also could not do given what he saw as an implicit contract with the city-state, according to which he had agreed to abide by the laws of Athens in exchange for the benefits of living there.

This was all in keeping with the life of *aretē*, or virtue, of fundamental concern to ancient philosophers concerned with pursuit of the good life. Socrates was committed to the pursuit of wisdom and was willing to be brought to court for doing so. He was also committed to justice and was willing to die on its account. It is important to acknowledge, however, that Socrates was challenging the justice of the court, not the law itself, which may sound incomplete to the ear of a modern social justice activist accustomed to a notion of civil disobedience that often challenges not only the court, but the law itself, as unjust.

How is this kind of "virtue" helpful to us?

The answer harks back to Socrates's insistence that he was providing a moral service to the city-state of Athens by asking challenging questions designed to test the wisdom of the supposed illuminati of Athenian society. This skeptical stance against persons of authority in Athens aligns well with the suspicions that Critical Social Justice brings to bear on persons of power and privilege, and the institutional authority they represent, in the modern world. Both Socrates and Critical Social Justice are inclined to question and challenge the norms, habits, practices, and beliefs that hold seat in the court of public opinion.

There is the additional challenge, however, of figuring out the best way to effectively advance the cause of social justice. Many people can be interested in social justice but not everyone usually agrees on what precisely constitutes social justice and how to go about putting it into effect. Indeed, vehement disagreements in the twenty-first century about the nature of social justice often degenerate into partisan vitriol. Moreover, the phenomenon known as "cancel culture," covered in chapter 2, refers to what many perceive as persecution campaigns against authors, speakers, politicians, professors, celebrities, and others who express a view deemed too controversial to tolerate, resulting in their exile, or "cancellation" (fired, shamed, or otherwise ostracized), from respectable society.

It is perhaps not a stretch of imagination, then, to suggest that the aplomb with which Socrates confronted the court in which he was tried on charges of impiety and corrupting Athenian youth, and ultimately his public censure and death sentence, can strike a chord with a modern reader concerned about the acrimonious and histrionic nature of disagreements about social justice activism. It can also strike a chord with readers concerned with how best to be of service to society in asking provocative questions about the nature of social justice and the extent to which social justice prevails in modern society. In both cases, we are dealing with the "court" of public opinion.

Do Socrates and the Stoic philosophers who came after him provide us with a guide for navigating the controversies of social justice activism that play out in the court of public opinion in the twenty-first century? Do they provide us with a guide for being better people who contribute to a better and more just society? Do they help us in our pursuit of well-being? The answer is yes.

How so? For Socrates and the Stoic philosophers who came after him, reason and virtue were core concerns in a commitment to intellectual inquiry that was not simply for mental stimulation. For them, reason and virtue were a way of life, a path to living a good life, depending fundamentally not on the circumstances of your life, but in the living of your life as virtuously as you can. The responsibility rests on you, but in relying on your capacity for reason and virtue, the point is not to see yourself as atomistic and alone, but as a contributing member of the human community. Stoicism is not irrelevant to contemporary social justice activism. In fact, it supplements and improves it.

CRITICAL THEORY

Social justice is nothing new, but the wave of social justice activism that arrived on the scene in the 2010s as a topic of widespread concern draws upon ideas from philosophers working in the "continental" tradition of Western philosophy. We will learn more about the history of these ideas in chapters 2 and 4, but for now we note that this tradition includes Frankfurt School philosophers such as Max Horkheimer and Theodor Adorno and postmodern philosophers like Michel Foucault and (as some might argue) Friedrich Nietzsche. In particular, the Frankfurt School philosophers were responsible for providing perhaps the earliest articulation of what is now known as Critical Theory, which has become the central framework for thinking about social justice in the twenty-first century.

The aim of Critical Theory is to study the social conditions and ramifications of what we know—e.g., how knowledge does or does not enable social inequality. Broadly conceived, Critical Theory can be traced back earlier to the ideas of Immanuel Kant and Georg Hegel, or even as far back to Socrates himself, but it coalesces explicitly in the Western Marxist tradition of the Frankfurt School, which was established in the first half of the twentieth century. The Frankfurt School included philosophers such as Max Horkheimer, Theodor Adorno, Walter Benjamin, Erich Fromm, Herbert Marcuse, and others. Signature works include the *Dialectic of Enlightenment* by Theodor Adorno and Max Horkheimer and *Eros and Civilization* by Herbert Marcuse.[4]

A central thesis, as articulated in the *Dialectic*, was that the Enlightenment's belief in reason and science as revelatory instruments that would liberate mankind from superstition, myth, and subservience to the brute whims of nature was not unlike religious faith in how it fell into "false consciousness," a subliminal obedience to an oppressive social order. In this work, Horkheimer and Adorno argued that the Enlightenment—a seventeenth- and eighteenth-century intellectual movement defined by its commitment to rationality and human autonomy, and specifically defined by Kant as man's emergence from self-imposed immaturity—had failed to prevent war and fascism.

It had also left people in modern society in a state of alienation. It had so heavily promoted technology, material progress, and scientific inquiry as foundational institutions that human life had degenerated into the "one-dimensional man" of capitalism, whereby people were so ideologically co-opted by Western capitalism (and the Communist Soviet Union) that they had become disinclined to, almost incapable of, critical thinking. Like feudalism and other past social orders, industrial capitalism imposed a uniformity on cultural life that severely hampered the potential for human liberation and the exercise of human imagination that the authors believed is essential to human happiness.

The cultural machinery of capitalism—consumerism, entertainment, industrialization, mass media—homogenized the populace into heedless agents of mass consumption and mass production. It molded them into *homo economicus* automatons rather than autonomous agents harvesting the fruits of their independence and creative potential. The business of a capitalist society is business, and this means that human autonomy is sacrificed on the altar of material progress, which in the age of industrial capitalism means that happiness stems from the "freedom" to buy goods and services. Aesthetic aspirations in the human imagination, iconoclastic ideas and idiosyncratic behavior that veer from the norms that characterize a society, are too subversive to fit neatly into the intricate web of interests that motivate the guardians of the status quo.

The *Dialectic* authors were writing when film, television, and radio were coming into their own as dominant venues for disseminating cultural messages. One might argue that the digital age has become too decentralized for corporate interests to consolidate control. But contemporary examples of cultural conformity abound.

Google search data and Amazon purchases, for example, can be converted into real-time advertisements on iPhones and laptops that exploit our propensity to buy the latest fads. Professional sports teams and leagues harness fan loyalties into millions of dollars of sales of team and league merchandise. Disney has a powerful brand that finds its way onto the Christmas wish list of children writing to Santa every December. Earnings seasons roil the markets with investor anxieties about whether growth in sales of the next generation of iPhones will meet expectations.

Meanwhile, industrial capitalism was dominant even in the arts. In the *Dialectic*'s fourth excursus, on the "culture industry," Adorno and Horkheimer write: "any trace of spontaneity from the public in official broadcasting is controlled and absorbed by talent scouts, studio competitions and official programs of every kind selected by professionals. Talented performers belong to the industry long before it displays them; otherwise they would not be so eager to fit in."[5] Performers become as interested in learning the business of their art as they are in mastering the art of their business.

This idea of cultural hegemony through cultural homogenization may strike readers as revolutionary when they first read the *Dialectic*, as well as the explanation they provided for how a whole society of people can become unwittingly subservient within an oppressive social order. Drawing a distinction between "instrumental" and "objective" reason, the authors define the former as the reasoning capacity used to determine the most effective means to achieve one's ends, while defining the latter as the reasoning capacity used to assess and articulate the intrinsic value of the ends themselves.

While the Stoics (as we will see) were concerned with living in harmony with nature, the aim of Enlightenment rationality was to explore, control, and dominate nature. In the name of science and progress, the burgeoning appeal of Enlightenment rationality had a profound cultural and philosophical impact, elevating our understanding of rationality as an instrument for controlling and manipulating the world as it is (e.g., training medical students to become plastic surgeons or oncologists), in contrast to rationality as an objective guide for thinking about how the world should be (should we be more concerned about nose jobs or curing cancer?).

Instrumental reason is concerned with the control of nature (figuring out a way to make prettier faces or to cure cancer). Objective reason is concerned with how and why we control it (should more resources be devoted to beautiful faces or curing cancer?). The former seeks to acquire its own vested interests. The latter seeks to understand whether those vested interests are, in fact, in our best interest.

According to the Frankfurt School, in the world of globalized capitalism, our rational faculties are focused primarily, if not exclusively, on figuring out the means to attain one's ends, rather than evaluating the ends themselves. To make their point, the authors of the *Dialectic* present the Homeric hero Odysseus as an allegorical representation of the modern bourgeois individual. The point is made concisely in a lecture, which became a paper, on the *Dialectic* by a former professor at the University of Pennsylvania, Curtis Bowman:

> Like the bourgeoisie of the capitalist world, Odysseus employs instrumental reason to advance his self-interest. This enables him to survive the mythological terrors of the ancient world. He sacrifices all else that he might desire and value, even his crew, all of whom die on the way back to Ithaca. And so he escapes the mythological world of his voyage. Yet what does he return to? An enlightened world of freedom and autonomy? No, he returns to his kingdom, resuming his place as ruler of his people. His odyssey is thus a voyage in which—to express a complicated matter in a simple formula—Odysseus oppressed resumes his place as Odysseus the oppressor.[6]

Odysseus never seriously wonders about the ethical underpinnings of the world in which he lives. He simply assumes the throne after a ten-year odyssey that takes him on a tour of the mythical world, and rules again. This is no different than the modern bourgeois individual who makes use of his intelligence to secure a job, take out a loan from a bank, start an enterprise or grow a business, or save up money for retirement. Both Odysseus and the modern bourgeois individual employ instrumental reason to succeed in a world by pursuing ends that they take for granted. There is rarely, if ever, a pause to wonder if the ends they pursue are worth the effort to attain them.

Surely, we need not repudiate a good job, entrepreneurial success, or a dignified retirement. But the *Dialectic* authors were convinced that instrumental reason was one of the primary ways by which capitalism supports an overarching system of exploitation in society. If everyone is concerned only with means and not with ends, they do not think too hard about how they pursue ends custom-made for them by a social order defined by exploitative relations between capital and labor. The result is that people "buy into" a system that keeps them blind to their subordination.

Enlightenment celebrates rationality as the way to free us from being dominated by nature and the outdated myths we once relied upon in our feeble attempt to control nature (e.g., offering sacrifices to the gods on Olympus). But if rationality is simply concerned with optimizing our status within a society defined by relations between capital and labor, the public interest becomes rigidly preoccupied with material living standards that enrich capitalists while keeping labor "happy."

The culmination of all this is alienation from ourselves and from other people. It is a condition in which the material conditions of life deceive us into thinking we are better off than we really are. There is little, if any, concern or consciousness that arises about the inherent justice of the social order in which the material conditions of life are enjoyed. Science and technology create the mirage of happiness from improved living standards while doing nothing to dissolve the social tension resulting from a division of resources between those who rule and those who are ruled.

In capitalism, the bourgeoisie focus only on the determination of means to preserve or enhance their standing within the existing social order. The basic institutions of private property, rule of law, and class identity endure without critical evaluation. The victory over nature is a victory for oppressors at the expense of the oppressed.

The owners of the means of production exploit workers by putting them to work while living off the profits derived from selling the goods workers produce. The worker is a slave to the unrelenting machine of profit generation. When he finds a job, he finds himself alienated from his labor because the goods he produces with his own hands are lifted from his hands, sold on the market, and returned to him in the form of a wage that seems hardly worth the effort. The division of labor relegates the worker to a cog in the industrial machine, giving him a wage while stripping him of the dignity and self-possession one gains by laying claim to the goods he produces, not to mention giving him little or no protection against long hard hours in a hot dusty sweatshop or the stale confines of a cubicle.

Exploitation, then, is a direct legacy of the Enlightenment. For Karl Marx, exploitation meant the extraction of "surplus value" from the worker and the resulting alienation of the proletariat. For the authors of the *Dialectic*, exploitation was manifest in a system of social relations among consumers, captains of industry and entertainment, and the fledgling artists co-opted by the institutions that force-feed the commodification of technological and artistic "progress" to the masses.

Material progress upholds and preserves the control of the titans over the fates of the fledgling artists who dream up deceptive fantasies of fame and fortune. This is not unlike restrictive social orders of old. Whether it is slavery in ancient societies, serfdom in medieval feudal orders, or spiritual indoctrination in religious societies, the keepers of customs ensure that members of a tribe or society adhere to the traditions that enrich and sustain the power of those who keep the customs.

Enlightenment was supposed to free mankind from myth, but instead it yielded a form of rationality that accommodated the mind of man to the ideology of a capitalist order that promised enhancements in material well-being in exchange for obedience, or at least accommodation, to the efficiencies of mass production. But those who own the means of production were the new keepers of a "culture industry" that enforces the compliance of the oppressed. Enlightenment had become like the myths it was supposed to uproot. In the process, it alienated us not only from each other, but from nature.

AUTONOMY AND ALIENATION

The central theme of the Frankfurt School was the contrast between autonomy and alienation in a world of industrial capitalism. Influenced by Immanuel Kant, they believed in rational autonomy. Influenced by Karl Marx, they attempted to show how capitalism undermined the cultivation of rational autonomy. They identified a distinction between instrumental reason and objective reason, the former centered on means over ends as we learn to live within the routines and norms of capitalism, the latter focused on whether the ends we pursue are inherently worthwhile.

In the modern world, instrumental reason had eclipsed objective reason. What matters in this world are things like the bottom line, timesheets, deadlines, paying bills, commuting routines, cubicles and offices, bosses, Excel spreadsheets, reports, emails, and performance expectations. These things all seem to lend credence to the key claim of Horkheimer and Adorno that the life of work and responsibility in modern society is all about alienation. One can easily feel a keen sense of dissatisfaction with the cares and concerns of adulthood in this hard-charging world of "capitalism."

But are these the avoidable cares and concerns of "capitalism" or the unavoidable cares and concerns of life in general? Admittedly, Excel and emails (for example) are modern inventions, unknown to first-generation Frankfurt School philosophers or people in previous generations preoccupied with their own cares and concerns. But part of one's maturation and comeuppance in any society is learning to acclimate to the constraints imposed by history and circumstance.

This is akin to what economists call *constrained optimization*.

While this phrase sounds fancy, it conveys a simple point: people seek to optimize within a set of constraints.

When people think of economists, they think of policy wonks who run the Treasury Department or the Federal Reserve, Wall Street whizzes who make lots of money, or professors who draw supply and demand curves on a whiteboard. At heart, however, economics applies to every aspect of life. Buying things in a store. Household production. Police shootings. Your personal identity. Deciding who to vote for. Deciding what to wear to a funeral. What to do about falling in love. In an important sense, life all comes down to the economics of cost-benefit analysis.

When you go to the store, you buy a product most suitable for you given prices, your preferences, and your budget. When running a household, you need to figure out not only how to complete chores efficiently, but how to allocate the time you spend with yourself and the time you spend with your family. Research on police shootings suggests that police officers are utility maximizers who consider the expected costs of officer-involved shootings.[7]

As for identity, George A. Akerlof and Rachel E. Kranton argue that "people's notions of what is proper, and what is forbidden, and for whom, are fundamental to how hard they work, and how they learn, spend, and save."[8] When going to the ballot, you choose the candidate you think is best, among the candidates available. When deciding what to wear to a funeral, you may find it necessary to dress up in a formal suit or, if you come from a more iconoclastic family, perhaps you are less worried about the style of your dress than whether you are prepared for the weather. When seeking romantic partners, you are constrained by income, interests, culture, social status, and location.

In each case, we do the best that we can, but must do so while working with the resources we have at hand. We *optimize*, within a given set of *constraints*. Economists are especially interested in how we do this *efficiently*, in a way that generates the most incremental value, or as the old saying goes, the biggest bang for the buck. It is in this sense that we might think of economists as drawn more toward instrumental reason rather than objective reason.

There is, however, a parallel to a Stoic way of thinking. As Professor John Sellars says in describing Stoicism as a naturalistic philosophy, there is a "strong strand of realism" in Stoicism. There are "facts of life" we cannot avoid. Professor Sellars is referring more philosophically to Stoicism as a "complete, integrated system" of thought that confronts head-on the reality that we cannot escape the natural process of change associated with birth, growing up, getting old, illness, and death.[9]

It is no stretch of imagination, however, to say that economies are like ecosystems, and that the resource constraints that "rational" consumers face in inherently dynamic economies are like the resource constraints that rational human beings face in inherently dynamic ecosystems. As explained by Pierre Hadot, author of *The Inner Citadel*, an in-depth and thoughtful examination of Marcus Aurelius's *Meditations*:

> Stoic Nature, like its Aristotelian counterpart, acts like a good administrator or craftsman, who gets the best she can from the available materials. . . . Reason demands a determinate, and therefore finite, object. The possibilities open to it are limited, and it must choose between quite determinate contrary solutions, each of which have their drawbacks and advantages.[10]

Some may detect a stark difference between Stoicism and the utilitarian, seemingly Epicurean (an ancient philosophical school, contemporary with the Stoics, which advocated that that pleasure should be our goal), ethic underlying economics. The former, as Sellars also notes, prioritizes process rather than outcome, while the latter seems to prioritize outcome rather than process.

For the Stoic, happiness depends on whether your pursuits are virtuous— whether you choose a course of action because it is virtuous, and not worrying so much about the outcome.[11] For the economist, happiness depends on whether you obtain your desired outcome. The economist is focused on the process only to the extent he is focused on obtaining the outcome in the most efficient way possible. The Stoic cares about objective reason. The economist cares about instrumental reason.

For the economist, then, preferences are taken for granted. It is simply assumed that people know what is best for them, with introspection a peripheral concern at best. The Stoic, however, can be said to be fundamentally interested in the introspection that precedes decision-making. As we will see in chapter 3, for the Stoics, the ideal life is one in which reason determines one's thoughts and actions such that they are anchored on four cardinal virtues which bring one into harmony with nature, or Logos. Pierre Hadot, in his analysis of the *Meditations*, sums it up nicely:

Stoicism is a philosophy of self-coherence, based on a remarkable intuition of
the essence of life. From the very first moment of its existence, every living
being is instinctively attuned to itself; that is, it tends to preserve itself, to love
its own existence, and to love all that can preserve this existence. This instinc-
tive accord becomes a moral accord with oneself, as soon as man discovers by
means of his reason that the supreme value is not those things which are the
objects of this instinct for self-preservation, but the reflective choice of accord
with oneself, and the *activity of choice itself*.[12]

"Philosophy," according to Hadot, "is not wisdom, but only the exercise
of wisdom." The goal of Stoic philosophy is "to allow the philosopher to
orient himself or herself within the uncertainties of daily life, by proposing
probable choices that our reason can accept, even if it is not always sure it
ought to."[13] The Stoic, like the economist, focuses on means, but unlike the
economist, focuses not on whether the means are efficient, but whether the
means are virtuous.

As an example, "the brave and generous," *Intelligent Virtue* author Julia
Annas writes, "do not merely have overall aims in their lives that turn out, as
a matter of fact, to be good. Rather, they have an attitude to goodness which
can be described as commitment: goodness attracts them in a way that the
vicious are not attracted, and the mediocre are attracted only weakly."[14]

"What matters," Hadot writes, "are not the results or efficiency, but the
intention to do good. What matters is to act out of one motive alone, without
any other considerations of interest or pleasure: that of the moral good. This
is the only value, and the only one we need."[15] We might fail to recognize,
however, that virtue and efficiency are not necessarily inconsistent. As philosopher Dirk Baltzly notes in the Stanford Encyclopedia of Philosophy, the
Stoics "draw a distinction between what is good and things that have value
(*axia*). Some indifferent things, like health or wealth, have value and therefore are to be preferred, even if they are not good, because they are typically
appropriate, fitting or suitable (*oikeion*) for us."[16] We can pursue goods that
have value (get the "biggest bang for the buck") as long as we do so virtuously. As Dirk Baltzly notes:

> it is rational *selection*—not the attainment of—these things which constitutes
> happiness. . . . From the point of view of happiness, the things according to
> nature are still indifferent. What matters for our happiness is whether we select
> them rationally and, as it turns out, this means selecting them in accordance with
> the virtuous way of regarding them (and virtuous action itself).[17]

This clarification invokes the key distinction made by Julia Annas between
the living of your life and the circumstances of your life. "On the *eudaimonist*
approach . . . neither virtue nor happiness is a matter of the circumstances of

my life. (This is consistent with the point that these circumstances might put constraints on happiness.) Both living virtuously and living happily are ways of living my life, dealing with the materials I have to hand, making the best of the life I have led up to now."[18] If happiness arises from virtue, it is because it arises "at least in part from the way we do or don't actively live our lives, doing something with them or acting in relation to them."[19]

Let's consider a matter involving life and death.

In a lecture on Marcus Aurelius's *Meditations*, Professor Michael Sugrue claims that the Stoic conception of virtue is in anticipation of the Kantian conception of virtue.[20] Among other things, Kant is famous for articulating what has come to be known as the *categorical imperative,* which roughly states that you should only act in such a way that, as a matter of rational judgment, your action should be elevated to the status of a universal moral law. An example includes the maxim that you should never lie.

However, as Pierre Hadot notes in likening the Stoic "community of rational beings" to Kant's "kingdom of ends,"[21] Kant also argued that you should only treat people as ends-in-themselves (beings capable of rational decision-making) rather than as means to an end (making decisions for them without obtaining their assent). If the Gestapo is at your door looking for Jews in the attic, you can make a plausible case for lying because otherwise you ensure your safety at the expense of the Jews hiding in your attic, who likely would not rationally assent to being discovered.[22]

You are acting in accord with virtue because, as philosopher Christine Korsgaard notes, "in evil circumstances, but only then, the Kingdom of Ends can become a goal to seek rather than an ideal to live up to."[23] It takes wisdom to distinguish between seeking the realization of an ideal and living up to an ideal. In seeking to realize this Kingdom of Ends, you are acting in accord with wisdom, justice, courage, and self-control. It takes rational judgment—wisdom—to discern when it is appropriate to lie. It takes courage and self-control to lie to the Gestapo in the interest of justice.

One may raise the obvious objection that lying is not virtuous per se. First, the Gestapo may not believe you if everyone else has been lying, thus undermining the pursuit of your goal in the first place. Second, lying to the Gestapo helps others escape the fear of death only momentarily (as chances of survival during Nazi occupation were not good), but not philosophically in the Stoic sense that it is a mistake in judgment to fear death. Ultimately, however, refusing to lie may ensure your safety at the expense of the Jews hiding in your attic, who likely would not rationally assent to being discovered.

As we can gather from Pierre Hadot in *The Inner Citadel*, however, this kind of dilemma turns on an understanding of how the Stoics conceived of value. It "is the problem that Marcus faced as Emperor: he had to seek the happiness of his subjects in the domain of indifferent things, which had no value in his eyes."[24] Only "things which are an integral part of 'life according to nature'" (i.e., virtue) are absolute. But there are "things which could help the practice of virtue in a secondary way." Health and wealth, for example, are things that "are neither good nor bad, but are indifferent with regard to moral good."[25][26]

Nonetheless, "possessing them and exercising them . . . allows us to practice better the virtuous life." Finally, there are "things which, under certain circumstances, could be useful to virtue." Health and wealth could, for example, allow "us to come to the aid of our fellow man."[27] If you are a healthy, well-heeled member of a city under Nazi control, you might use your status to protect and provide for Jews in hiding, while lying to the Gestapo as circumstances necessitate.

As Dirk Baltzly explains, "there will be times when the circumstances make it rational . . . to select something that is (generally speaking) contrary to [your] nature."[28]

The autonomous person who acts wisely uses reason to discern the moral action he is obliged to undertake within the set of constraints imposed on him. The Gestapo at the door is a serious, life-altering constraint that must be handled carefully while attempting to preserve the lives of the Jews. The most efficient, and virtuous, thing to do may be to lie. If you do, you serve the cause of justice (also acting wisely and courageously, while relying on one's self-control to remain poised) and are alienated from neither nature nor the human community, which, for the Stoics, are one and the same thing. Instead, you are a person who realizes autonomy in the exercise of reason.

> the Stoic delimits a center of autonomy—the soul, as opposed to the body; and a guiding principle (*hêgemonikon*) as opposed to the rest of the soul. It is within this guiding principle that freedom and our true self are located. It is also there, and only there, that moral good and evil can be found, for the only moral good and evil are voluntary good and evil.[29]

THE NATURE OF REASON

Here we arrive at a crucial point. A disciple of the Frankfurt School might say the economist is focused on instrumental reason, while the Stoic is focused on objective reason. That is, the economist is concerned with means without thinking too hard about the reasonableness of ends, while the Stoic is concerned with the reasonableness (strictly speaking, the virtue) of *both* the means *and* the ends.

The Stoic believes happiness stems from virtue. If you choose to do something for its own sake because it is virtuous, your choice implies that the end (e.g., a just outcome) is also virtuous—i.e., it is inherently valuable. For example, writes Julia Annas, "to become brave requires you to accept that some things, and not others, are valuable in your life," which also implies that "your life has acquired a shape it did not have before your character developed in this way."[30]

For the economist, the means are "valuable" if they are efficient at obtaining the outcome, and it is simply assumed the outcome is valuable (makes you happy) because otherwise you would not pursue it. For the Stoic, the means are "valuable" if they are virtuous, regardless of whether you obtain the outcome. "Virtuous activity," writes Julia Annas, "may well be valued instrumentally for what it enables the person to do, but if it is virtuous it is also valued for itself."[31]

You prefer to obtain the outcome, but your happiness does not depend on it. Julia Annas writes: "Like the master craftsperson the virtuous person experiences enjoyment and satisfaction in her activity and not just in the result."[32] In other words, alienation does not *necessarily* follow from the "eclipse" of objective reason by instrumental reason. In fact, instrumental and objective reason do not have to come into conflict at all.

For the Stoic, the fundamental question is not whether you have determined that the ends you pursue are inherently "valuable," but whether reason guides you to an understanding of the virtue that underlies your choices. This stems from a naturalistic conception of the world in which, as Hadot writes, the "coherence with oneself is . . . based on the self-coherence of universal Reason or Nature."[33] Max Horkheimer would seem to agree:

Plato, for instance, undertakes in his *Republic* to prove that he who lives in the light of objective reason also lives a successful and happy life. The theory of objective reason did not focus on the coordination of behavior and aim, but on concepts—however mythological they sound to us today—on the idea of the greatest good, on the problem of human destiny, and on the way of realization of ultimate goals. There is a fundamental difference between this theory, according to which reason is a principle inherent in reality, and the doctrine that reason is a subjective faculty of the mind.

In Platonism, the Pythagorean theory of numbers, which originated in astral mythology, was transformed into the theory of ideas that attempts to define the supreme content of thinking as an absolute objectivity ultimately beyond, though related to, the faculty of thinking. *The present crisis of reason consists fundamentally in the fact that at a certain point thinking either became incapable of conceiving such objectivity at all or began to negate it as a delusion* [emphasis mine].[34]

Like Platonists, the Stoics also saw the universe as a kind of "absolute objectivity." For the Stoics, however, the "supreme content of thinking" did not transcend "the faculty of thinking." Rather, the faculty of thinking, or reason, was part of the "absolute objectivity" of nature, or Logos, of which we are a part.

"The Stoics," writes Emily Wilson in her biography of Seneca, "challenged the view common among other philosophical movements in antiquity (such as Platonism) that the human soul includes both rational and irrational elements. For them, human beings are a complete whole, not a collection of diverse parts, and that whole is entirely rational—although people are prone to false reasoning and mistaken beliefs."[35]

Reason is vital. The distinction between instrumental and objective reason is useful, but not because they necessarily come into conflict. Instead, it is because the distinction helps illuminate that they must work together if reason is to reach its full potential—to align our thoughts and actions with nature. "The Stoics," Emily Wilson explains, "believed that the whole world is governed by universal Reason or Fate or God or Providence, also identified as Jupiter or Zeus, and associated with the primordial Fire, which guides all of nature."[36] We should thus "follow nature, because nature is always good," which leads to an emphasis on "individual decisions, since we always have a choice about whether we conform our will to the will of the universe, or resist."[37]

The Frankfurt School was particularly critical of the early twentieth-century school of logical positivism, which argued that statements are meaningful only if they can be logically or empirically verified. In emphasizing the importance of logical reasoning, the Frankfurt School philosophers feared that logical positivism reinforced the kind of modern scientific reasoning that underpins industrial capitalism, while simultaneously ignoring, even belittling, the kind of "speculative" philosophy concerned with meaning, morality, and the value we attach to our actions.

This is not to take a detour into logical positivism, but to point out that if we are not careful, the Frankfurt School's critique of instrumental reason, as well as logical positivism, can mislead us into overlooking the vital importance of logical reasoning as a means of gaining knowledge about nature and virtue. Indeed, logic was vital to Stoicism, along with physics and ethics. As described by Émile Bréhier, quoted by Pierre Hadot:

It is one single, unique reason which, in dialectics, links consequent propositions to their antecedents; which, in nature, links together all causes; and which, in human conduct, establishes perfect concord between acts. It is impossible that a good man should not be a physicist and a dialectician; it is impossible for rationality to be realized separately in these three areas; it is impossible completely to grasp the reason within the course of events in the universe with-out, at the same time, realizing reason within one's own behavior.[38]

It would be a mistake to say the Frankfurt School would have us do away with math, science, and logical thinking, although some passages about sci-ence and mathematical reasoning within the *Dialectic* risk veering into such silliness. The point is that logic is one of the three main, interrelated fields of inquiry in Stoic philosophy (along with physics and ethics). Logic is essential in our quest for knowledge, and because *eudaimonia* (happiness) depends crucially on virtue, "virtue and knowledge are . . . closely connected,"[39] which by extension makes logic—and instrumental reasoning—essential to human autonomy. We will learn about the importance of physics, logic, and ethics in Stoicism in chapter 3.

NOT A COG IN THE MACHINE

Virtue and efficiency do not always, or necessarily, come into conflict. With this realization in mind, we can see that the "market" economy is not inher-ently compromised by "alien" forces of hegemonic control exerted by status quo custodians who deny us happiness while dispensing with conventional wisdom that upholds the ideologies of capitalism, keeping everyone in a state of unwitting oppression.

With reason as a guide to life, we do not necessarily "sell out" or "give in" to oppression by working within the so-called status quo, resigned to a Sisyphean life of alienation made unavoidable by the structural impediments of "capitalism." Instead, one can learn how to think more insightfully and live more confidently by gaining a clearer understanding of society and how to live within it.

The key is to think in terms of constrained optimization. The framework of constrained optimization is the basis of what some claim to be the "imperi-alistic" approach of economics (i.e., the approach can be used to study many aspects of human life). As Nobel Laureate Gary Becker wrote, the notion of maximizing behavior with stable preferences, in the context of "prices and other market instruments [that] allocate the scarce resources within a society and thereby constrain the desires of participants and coordinate their actions," is a robust approach to the study of all human behavior.[40]

This approach, or perspective, is like a philosophy of life. Stoic author and psychotherapist Donald Robertson implicitly invokes this framework when discussing the importance of "evaluating the consequences of desires." The idea is that cost-benefit analysis—the essence of a constrained optimization framework—urges us to "weigh the consequences (for example) of following the desire (a bad habit) against those of exercising moderation or doing something else."

It is, in fact, akin to the dichotomy of control, articulated by the Roman Stoic Epictetus: "There are things which are within our power, and there are things which are beyond our power" (*Enchiridion*, I). As a creature of reason, we have the power to judge the value of the ends we pursue and the most virtuous, and efficient, way to go about obtaining them, without getting too worked up about whether we obtain them. If so, then there may be something amiss in the notion that "structural" impediments such as "capitalist ideology" in postindustrial society have some necessary relation to alienation, or in social justice terms, a feeling of oppression or dissatisfaction with the status quo.

Let's take another example.

In January 2019, the American Psychological Association (APA) issued a new guidance document.[41] The APA document cited research suggesting that "the study of men need[s] the same gender-aware approach" that has been applied to the study of women, and that "the main thrust of the subsequent research is that traditional masculinity—marked by *stoicism*, competitiveness, dominance and aggression—is, on the whole, harmful."[42]

The guidelines acknowledge that they "may not be applicable to every professional and clinical situation" and that they "are not definitive and are designed to respect the decision-making judgment of individual professional psychologists."[43] Nonetheless, many worried that discursive currents in the Critical Social Justice movement, which we examine and describe in more detail in the next chapter, had imbued "traditional" masculinity with an ideological taint that focuses on social-cultural-historical "constructs" as sources of oppression and marginalization.

Indeed, the first guideline states that "psychologists strive to recognize that masculinities are constructed based on social, cultural, and contextual norms." Moreover, "traditional masculinity ideology can be viewed as the dominant (referred to as 'hegemonic') form of masculinity that strongly influences what members of a culture take to be normative."[44] As we will see in the next chapter, social constructivism is a key aspect of Critical Social Justice activism and scholarship.

The notion of masculinity as a set of socially constructed norms is not wrong, but it has become so prevalent a shortcut for societal analysis that it risks succumbing to the shortcomings of confirmation bias. It becomes not a framework but a dogma, a kind of ideological imperialism that shoehorns every situational intricacy into its conceptual framework for understanding not only masculinity (and other social phenomena) in general, but any aspect of masculinity at issue in any given situation.

These concerns are not about being opposed to scrutinizing "masculine" norms that may be harmful to the mental health of men. Moreover, it is true that the APA guidelines are not meant to be rigidly applied to every clinical situation, though Ronald F. Levant, professor emeritus of psychology at the University of Akron and co-editor of the APA volume "The Psychology of Men and Masculinities," is quoted as saying: "Though men benefit from patriarchy, they are also impinged upon by patriarchy."[45] Patriarchy is one of the "social constructs" frequently targeted by social justice activists as being associated with traditional masculinity.

There is, however, good reason to be dismayed by the strong influence that social justice ideology exerted on the report. As noted in an essay published by the Good Men Project, the APA guidelines seemed "to be hitching [their] wagon to the hidebound focus of social justice ideology on historical-social constructivism and dismantling 'power structures' while glossing over the nuances and situational intricacies of the lived experiences of men."[46] Much of the unease among critics of the contemporary social justice movement arises from this obsession with social constructivism.

It is not as if there is no merit to political activism that goes about trying to dismantle "patriarchal" structures that may undermine the mental health of men or impede progress in the attainment of equal opportunity for women. Indeed, as Professor Anthony Long emphasized at the 2018 Stoicon, Stoicism is itself a "public philosophy" that "was designed for action in the world," as shown by the admiration reserved among the Stoic philosophers for Socrates and Cato.[47]

However, Professor Long also notes in a podcast interview with Massimo Pigliucci that, among sociologists, "there's a tendency to explain everything today in the outer world in terms of social movements." But it is people who make decisions. Even if decisions are made collectively, each person is an individual with reason, which makes possible the ability to make decisions. Agency is among the most important principles of Stoicism. Each person is responsible for his own decisions. He may be part of society, but he has the capacity to make decisions. He is not a cog in a machine.[48]

CRITICAL SOCIAL JUSTICE AND LIBERAL HUMANISM

Among the ideas that have gained currency in social justice discourse is the notion that how we understand the nature and role of human reason is necessarily wrapped up in historical circumstances and should not automatically be trusted as an effective tool in arriving at an objective assessment of injustice. As Max Horkheimer wrote:

Reason cannot become transparent to itself as long as men act as members of an organism which lacks reason. Organism as a naturally developing and declining unity cannot be a sort of model for society, but only a form of deadened existence from which society must emancipate itself.[49]

Robin DiAngelo and Özlem Sensoy, authors of *Is Everyone Really Equal? An Introduction to Key Concepts in Social Justice Education*, put it rather imprecisely in claiming that "Critical Theory developed in part as a response to [the] presumed superiority and infallibility of scientific method, and raised questions about whose rationality and whose presumed objectivity underlies scientific methods."[50] The point was not to relegate reason to a matter of mere perspective. It was not relativism, but politics and historical moment, that motivated Critical Theory.

As Max Horkheimer writes, "no theory of society, even that of the sociologists concerned with general laws, does not contain political motivations, and the truth of these must be decided not in supposedly neutral reflection but in personal thought and action, in concrete historical activity."[51]

DiAngelo and Sensoy write that Critical Theory was a reaction to the scientific method and positivism, which "rested on the importance of reason, principles of rational thought, the infallibility of close observation, and the discovery of natural laws and principles governing life and society."[52] As noted, Horkheimer and Adorno were not favorably disposed to logical positivism. But they were responding to a specific philosophical school that they viewed as reinforcing the mindset of instrumental reason in a capitalistic society. Moreover, in *Eclipse of Reason* and *Dialectic of Enlightenment*, their target was science as an exploitative instrument of industrial capitalism. It was not the devaluation of reason, but the perversion of reason, that was of primary concern.

As we will see in chapter 3, doubts about the interplay between reason and society conflict with the Stoic view of human communities as immanent within a universe animated by reason. At the same time, when people assent to incorrect judgments about the world around them, it would seem to be the case that Stoicism shares the concern of social justice discourse that reason, when not well-developed or well-used, may not necessarily bring society into alignment with justice.

In contemporary discourse, however, Critical Social Justice (which is a specific approach to social justice to be explored in the next chapter) takes aim not at Stoicism, but at liberal humanism. Critical Social Justice seeks to navigate the norms and beliefs that organically situate people into hierarchical systems stratified by race, gender, sexual orientation, and other social identities. In the words of Helen Pluckrose, coauthor of the book *Cynical Theories*, liberalism "generally reject[s] this reductionist worldview and seek[s] to overcome racism, sexism, and homophobia by consistently objecting to anybody's worth being evaluated by their race, sex or sexuality and seeking empirical evidence of discrimination and effective ways to overcome it."[53]

Admittedly, liberal humanism is a kind of catch-all term that is hard to define. Some argue it is a "myth" referring to a belief in the "imperial ideology and mission" of Enlightenment philosophies such as rationalism, empiricism, and utilitarianism. These philosophies focus on individual rights, democratic principles, constitutional governments, and "bourgeois" values like rationality and laissez-faire markets.

As Rutgers University English Professor M. A. Rafey Habib argues:

> Liberal humanism is not so simply and easily to be defined. Liberal humanism has included both formalism and historicism, both scientism and moralism, both rationalism and empiricism, both objectivism and subjectivism. The commonly held view of liberal humanism—as harboring fixed notions of identity, the human subject, an independent external world, and as affirming that language represents reality—is a myth. It sets up a straw target. These notions are not principles of bourgeois thought: they are Medieval conceptions, going back to Plato and Aristotle, and they were already beginning to be challenged in the Renaissance. It was the very task of the bourgeois thinkers themselves to undermine these conceptions. There is no conception of a stable human self or ego in bourgeois philosophy: for Locke, the self was a blank slate, acquiring character only as experience writes on it; for Hume, it is a convention; for Kant, it is a mere presupposition; for Hegel, it is a product of historical forces and reciprocation with other human selves, which are equally constructed.[54]

The suggestion seems to be that liberal critics of Critical Social Justice ironically and unwittingly set up their own "liberal humanism" as a straw man by committing to an ill-defined "Enlightenment rationality" that they believe Critical Social Justice assails. This claim is an interesting twist that is relevant as we consider Stoicism as an alternative to Critical Social Justice.

The point is that the controversies about social justice in the early twenty-first century boil down to a conflict between those focused on reforming a liberal status quo but vigorously defending its foundations, and those focused on reforming, but also questioning and perhaps even overturning, values and institutions that underlie the liberal status quo. For example, Richard Delgado and Jean Stefancic write in their introduction to *Critical Race Theory: An Introduction*:

> Unlike traditional civil rights discourse, which stresses incrementalism and step-by-step progress, critical race theory questions the very foundations of the liberal order, including equality theory, legal reasoning, Enlightenment rationalism, and neutral principles of constitutional law.[55]

The conflict is about how we think about the historical circumstances in which we find ourselves, and the extent to which we believe these circumstances—manifested in institutional practices of law, education, business, politics, and entertainment—must change if justice is to prevail. The presumption of Critical Social Justice is that the well-being of people in society depends crucially on how they are affected by the social circumstances in which they were born. "Starting from the premise that a culture constructs its own social reality in ways that promote its own self-interest," write Delgado and Stefancic in *Critical Race Theory: The Cutting Edge*, critical race scholars "set out to construct a different reality."[56]

A subfield within the broader set of Critical Social Justice academic disciplines, critical race theory urges us to "not acquiesce in arrangements that are unfair and one-sided," and by "writing and speaking against them," one of the main techniques being storytelling and counter-storytelling, "we may hope to contribute to a better, fairer world."[57] Activism aimed at overturning unjust social arrangements and contributing to a better, fairer world certainly overlaps with the Stoic conception of justice as a virtue rooted in our nature as social creatures. But there is a crucial difference.

Critical Social Justice embraces an ethic based on a collectivist, sectarian paradigm of identity politics. People may be individuals who can attempt to optimize their well-being within these circumstances, but *the emphasis is on the circumstances that constrain their choices and actions rather than on the choices they make and the actions they undertake in response to these circumstances*. One might say that Critical Social Justice, unlike Stoicism, tends to see people as cogs in a machine.

THE DICHOTOMY OF CONTROL

The Critical Social Justice paradigm comes into conflict with one of the most fundamental principles of Stoicism. This principle is the "dichotomy of control" as articulated by a Roman Stoic named Epictetus. As Epictetus says in the first pages of his *Enchiridion* (Manual): "There are things which are within our power, and there are things which are beyond our power. Within our power are opinion, aim, desire, aversion, and . . . whatever affairs are our own. Beyond our power are body, property, reputation, office, and . . . whatever are not properly our own affairs" (*Enchiridion*, I).

How are we able to determine what is in our control and what is not? "Reason," Epictetus explains, "is unique among the faculties assigned to us in being able to evaluate itself—what it is, what it is capable of, how valuable it is—in addition to passing judgment on others" (*Discourses*, Book I, 1, 4). For the Stoics, the key to a well-lived life—*eudaimonia*, variously translated as "happiness," "flourishing," "fulfillment," "well-being," or the "good life"[58]— is to use accordingly what nature has given us.

The most important endowment we have received from nature is reason, the faculty by which we learn to make sound judgments of the sensations which impress themselves on the body as representations of the external world. "Men are disturbed not by things," Epictetus tells us, "but by the views which they take of things" (*Enchiridion*, V). We are disturbed not by the things that happen to us, or the circumstances in which we find ourselves. Instead, we are disturbed by *the judgment at which we arrive about* the things that happen to us within the circumstances in which we find ourselves.

This framework is constructed from a conception of human life as coterminous with the natural order of a corporeal universe in which reason is central as an organizing principle. We will learn more about the three themes of Stoic philosophical inquiry—physics, ethics, and logic—and how they interconnect in chapter 3. The basic idea is that the central aim of human life is to cultivate the capacity of reason to form objectively true perceptions of reality in the interest of developing a good moral character anchored on four cardinal virtues: wisdom, temperance, courage, and justice.

If we can harvest an "inner discourse" in the faculty of reason so that reason assents only to judgments about our sense impressions that correctly correspond to objective reality, we are on the path to *eudaimonia*, anchored on the "inner citadel" of a virtuous character living in the light of reason.[59]

While the Stoics conceive of one's character in absolute terms as either good or bad rather than in terms of gradations (i.e., the question is whether one is virtuous or not, not whether he is more or less virtuous today than yesterday, or more or less virtuous than another person), they also view the "Stoic sage" to be rare as a phoenix; in the words of the Roman Stoic Seneca, he "springs into existence . . . only once in five hundred years" (*Letter* 42).

Practically, then, the aim of reason might be said to be the pursuit of better judgment rather than perfect judgment. In the words of René Brouwer, the Stoic conception of progress refers "to the progress that someone makes towards wisdom, while still being in a state of inferiority."[60] This means learning how to bring our thoughts and actions in alignment with nature as effectively as our own character permits. If we do, we are on the path to *eudaimonia*, the well-lived life, benefiting ourselves and society. As Seneca writes:

> Is there no happiness immediately below wisdom? I think not. Because though he who makes progress is still among the fools, he is separated from them by a long interval (*Letter* 75).

As a note of clarification, bringing our thoughts and actions in alignment with nature, i.e., living in harmony with nature, presupposes an understanding of

nature among the ancients that is not necessarily synonymous with our contemporary understanding of nature. For the Stoics, a life that is in harmony
with nature is one that has achieved the highest state of perfection of which
it is capable. Nature is a teleological concept indicating the potential within
us to optimize the use of reason and to live virtuously, with each of us doing
so in a way that reflects our unique individual characteristics and capabilities.

Take emotions. In layman terms, (lower-case) stoicism is typically meant
to denote emotional repression. Think of the stiff upper lip of an aristocratic
Englishman in a Jane Austen novel. But this is not what the philosophy of
(upper-case) Stoicism encourages. As Professor John Sellars notes, "emotion" is the word given to the Greek *pathē* in translation, but "*pathē*" has
a narrower conception than "emotion" has for us in modern society.[61] It is
more akin to passion. We are susceptible to physiological impulses, or "first
movements," in immediate reaction to external stimuli like scratching an itch
after a mosquito bite. For the Stoics, emotions are the product of judgments
we make about these experiences after some time has elapsed and we are able
to think about them.

As Seneca writes:

> You must not think that our human virtue transcends nature; the wise man will
> tremble, will feel pain, will turn pale, because all these are sensations of the
> body. Where, then, is the home of our distress, of that which is truly evil? In
> the other part of us, no doubt, it is the mind that these trials drag, with force
> enough to cause to regret. The wise man, indeed, overcomes fortune by his
> virtue. (*Letter* 71)

Should we curse the mosquito, as if the mosquito had a personal vendetta
against us? Of course not. The mosquito is acting according to its nature. It
is so constituted that it seeks to consume human blood for sustenance. It is
an annoyance to human beings. But it is a "negative" emotion to get mad
about it. Once the itch goes away, we can forget about the mosquito and carry
on with our lives. However, what if we live in a part of the world in which
mosquitos carry and easily transmit malaria? The appropriate response is not
anger or fear. It is to seek treatment from competent doctors.

The Stoics teach us to judge emotions correctly, not incorrectly repress
emotions. We are encouraged to evaluate whether an emotion is positive or
negative. Reason gives us the capacity to distinguish between the benefit of
a wise reaction (seek treatment for malaria) and the cost of a foolish reaction
(lingering anger from getting bit, which saps energy and distracts us from
other aspects of our lives). An "emotion," then, is to be distinguished from
normal physiological responses like crying in grief over the sudden death
of a loved one. Emotions are the products of value judgments. If we feel

debilitated and incapacitated by our grief several years after the death of a loved one, we have failed to come to terms with death, a phenomenon that is a part of nature that we all experience in our lives.

In her book *Stoicism and Emotion*, Margaret Graver provides further clarification: "it will often be necessary for us to uphold a distinction between felt sensations in themselves and felt sensations as produced by particular kinds of judgment; in effect, between what it *feels like* to be afraid and what it *is* to be afraid."[62] The principle is elegantly articulated by the seventeeth-century Dutch (and Stoic-like) philosopher Baruch Spinoza, who wrote in *The Ethics*, "true virtue is nothing other than to live only by the guidance of reason, and so weakness consists solely in this, that a man suffers himself to be led by things external to himself and is determined by them to act in a way required by the general state of external circumstances, not by his own nature considered only in itself."[63]

STOICISM, CRITICAL SOCIAL JUSTICE, AND RATIONALITY

Sticking with mosquitoes, we can think of various reactions to a bite: getting mad, scratching an itch, or seeking treatment if symptoms arise that indicate a serious affliction such as malaria. If you find yourself in a hospital, you may find yourself thinking about less fortunate areas of the world in which mosquitoes regularly pose the threat of not only an itch but also of malaria.

You may be inclined to applaud the efforts of former U.S. President George W. Bush in launching the U.S. President's Malaria Initiative (PMI) in 2005. According to Malaria No More, PMI has "has been a lead contributor to global efforts that have saved more than 7 million lives and prevented more than 1 billion malaria cases since 2000."[64] You might even start looking at job postings to see what opportunities are available to help.

This is the kind of reaction a practicing Stoic may be inclined to undertake. It might also be expected that a contemporary social justice activist would have a similar reaction. One difference that may arise, however, is in how one is inclined to think about the underlying causes of malaria as a health crisis that needs our attention. A scholar with an eye on social justice as fundamentally an institutional matter may be inclined to explore the historical development of medical science and treatment in regions of the world that were historically subject to colonial rule.

In so doing, this scholar may produce valuable research on the relations between conquest, development, and health in Africa, as well as the current state of medical services in Africa, the marginalization of African healing, and the ethics of medical research and experimentation in colonial Africa.

An examination of this history of European empires in sub-Saharan Africa, writes Dr. Helen Tilley in the *AMA Journal of Ethics,* "highlights the extramedical factors that have affected health and healing across the continent. Military conquest and economic development were justified on the grounds that they would improve conditions for people in Africa and yet, in many places, they caused considerable harm."[65] For example, "there were . . . instances when health administrators decided that the uncertain effects of an intervention outweighed the possible benefits." With respect to malaria:

> Both immunological and ethical concerns, for instance, drove debates about malaria control and eradication across tropical Africa from the 1930s onward. Would it be right, several leading malariologists asked, to attempt eradication when doing so would interrupt the forms of immunity people acquired through a lifetime of exposure and failure would create the possibility for widespread pandemics, especially in areas of intense endemicity? Those who answered yes saw the issue as a question of short-versus long-term trade-offs: in their eyes, infant and child mortality from malaria, which in places in the early 1950s approached 25 percent of all childhood malaria cases, was already too high a cost to bear.

> Ultimately, the potential risks and logistical challenges proved too daunting; Africa was largely left out of the World Health Organization's global malaria eradication campaign (MEP), and a range of smaller pilot studies were initiated instead. By the mid-1960s, the global campaign had failed, leading to resurgent malaria in many parts of the developing world in which eradication had been attempted. Having been largely bypassed by the MEP, most African countries faced no such resurgence, but neither did they benefit from decreases in childhood mortality. For some, Africa's omission was thought to be not just the wisest but also the most ethical path. For others, such an omission was yet another example of neglect, lost opportunities, and ethical disregard.[66]

This history can be illuminating in helping us to understand the legacy of European imperialism. It can illustrate the complex interplay of interests and concerns that are at work within a given set of historical circumstances. Historical analysis with attention toward structural and institutional factors underlying inequities can provide a benchmark by which to compare and examine whether contemporary medical practices are improving upon the past. It can galvanize international efforts like PMI, which seems to be a marked improvement over coordinated efforts in the past.

The example of malaria brings together the various themes to be explored in this book. Mosquitoes carrying malaria are part of nature but represent a threat to human health. They are what the Stoics would call an "external" to ourselves as rational beings interacting with the natural world, but also a part of our nature in the sense that they interact with our blood, skin, and physiology.

The question then arises: how do we react? Self-preservation being our most basic instinct, we obviously set to work seeking treatment or, in an earlier historical era, finding a cure. As rational beings born into human societies in which no man is an island, we also should find it within ourselves to find a way to ensure that everyone has access to affordable treatment if stricken by malaria. That is, we have an instinct for both our physical and our moral self-preservation.

It seems safe to say that Stoics and social justice activists, in addition to many if not most others, can agree. But as a general matter, how are we to think about justice? Alternatively, since justice is one of four cardinal virtues for the Stoics, how are we to think about virtue? In answering these questions, we can gain insight into how we might rationally activate and make use of the native potential in all of us to make the world a better place, for ourselves and our fellow human beings.

VIRTUE SIGNALING

One glaring aspect of this native potential over the last decade, and in the last half-century of intellectual developments that now shape this impulse, is the way we talk about virtue—or justice. It has not been a discourse of harmony and consensus. Instead, we have witnessed a widening political divide between those on the Left and those on the Right about what counts as acceptable (virtuous) discourses, policies, and social norms. Critics of social justice orthodoxy often find themselves in the crosshairs of activists and scholars who would rather do without critique as they work relentlessly toward advancing an agenda that they believe is in the interest of justice.

One main result of this divide has been "cancel culture"—in brief, the idea that authors, speakers, politicians, professors, celebrities, and others should be "canceled" after expressing a view deemed too controversial to tolerate by partisans, left-wing or right-wing, strongly opposed to the view expressed.

For example, Peter Boghossian, coauthor of *How to Have Impossible Conversations*,[67] recently resigned from his position as Assistant Professor of Philosophy at Portland State University. After an academic career in which he "invited a wide range of guest lecturers to address my classes, from Flat-Earthers to Christian apologists to global climate skeptics to Occupy Wall Street advocates . . . not because I agreed with their worldviews, but primarily because I didn't," Boghossian resigned in large part because he increasingly "witnessed students refusing to engage with different points of view."

Moreover, "questions from faculty at diversity trainings that challenged approved narratives were instantly dismissed," and "those who asked for evidence to justify new institutional policies were accused of microaggressions," while "professors were accused of bigotry for assigning canonical texts written by philosophers who happened to have been European and male."[68] While it is true that Boghossian resigned and was not terminated, his resignation was the culmination of several years of working in a campus climate characterized by ideological homogeneity among faculty and students, while receiving minimal, if any, support from the administration.

In July 2020, 152 artists, activists, professors, and writers signed an open letter in *Harper's Magazine* decrying "a new set of moral attitudes and political commitments that tend to weaken our norms of open debate and toleration of differences in favor of ideological conformity."[69] In a two-week period from May 13, 2021, to May 28, 2021, *Areo Magazine* ran a series of articles about the importance of free speech in an age of cancel culture, as well as crackdowns on free speech and political freedom in countries like China.

These efforts are primarily a response to social media mobs, militant student activism, and media campaigns that effectively attempt to exile people from respectable society for running afoul of new rules on acceptable discourse. Not all of this is bad. During the #MeToo movement, people like Harvey Weinstein, Matt Lauer, and Charlie Rose deserved to be "canceled" for their serious offenses like rape and/or sexual harassment.

But did Harvard psychologist and linguist Steven Pinker deserve to be reprimanded by colleagues who called for his removal from the Linguistic Society of America's list of "distinguished academic fellows and media experts" because he "tends to 'move' in 'the proximity' of what one newspaper 'called' a revival of scientific racism" even though "the signatories do not accuse Pinker of 'scientific racism' with the attendant obligation to substantiate the charge"?[70]

As a famous and tenured scholar, Pinker was in no danger of being "canceled" for a few arguably careless tweets, but as *Atlantic* journalist Conor Friedersdorf notes, the signatories "did send a message to less powerful scholars that certain opinions, publicly stated, could result in professional sanction," which "wouldn't be cause for alarm if the speech in question were obviously and egregiously improper; if it consisted, for example, of racial slurs or open bigotry." Instead, "the hundreds of academics who targeted Pinker were not merely reaffirming sensible, widely agreed upon taboos. They were trying to radically narrow the bounds of acceptable speech and inquiry."[71]

Cancellation efforts come not only from the Left, but from the Right, as evidenced by the difficulties Colin Kaepernick has faced finding a job as an NFL quarterback ever since he decided to kneel during the playing of the national anthem. More recently, a young reporter named Emily Wilder was fired by the Associated Press after the Stanford College Republicans criticized her social media posts on the Israeli–Palestinian conflict and her "history of activism for Palestinian human rights."[72] When *New York Times* reporter Nikole Hannah-Jones was denied tenure in her position as a professor in the University of North Carolina's journalism school, some wondered if she had been canceled, particularly in light of her stewardship of the controversial 1619 Project.

Cancel culture is only one manifestation of these controversies, but it illustrates the potential for dire consequences for people who express views that run afoul of "acceptable" discourse among "polite" society in social circles on the Right and on the Left. Can Stoicism help the "victims" of cancel culture? Can it tell us something about social justice, debate over which is a source of many of the controversies leading to "cancellation" efforts? Can it change the way many currently think about social justice? Can Stoicism help us navigate the controversies that have emerged about the nature of social justice in the 2010s, and now the 2020s?

The answer is yes.

One indication goes back to the suggestion that liberal humanism is a myth. In the words of Professor Habib, liberal humanism does not harbor "fixed notions of identity, the human subject, an independent external world," and the belief "that language represents reality." As Habib writes, "these notions are not principles of bourgeois thought: they are Medieval conceptions, going back to Plato and Aristotle, and they were already beginning to be challenged in the Renaissance." He adds that "it was the very task of the bourgeois thinkers themselves to undermine these conceptions," as "there is no conception of a stable human self or ego in bourgeois philosophy."[73]

This claim takes on plausibility if we consider Stoic author Donald Robertson's remark in a podcast conversation with fellow Stoic author John Sellars that the popularity of Stoicism reflects a reaction to Enlightenment rationality and the separation between mind and body in modern Western thought. As we have seen above, alienation is a major theme in modern critiques of Enlightenment rationality. As Robertson notes, the Roman Emperor and Stoic philosopher Marcus Aurelius was committed to the idea of overcoming alienation from nature and mankind.[74]

Doing so is a key feature of the Stoic view that we must think of ourselves as part of a greater whole—nature and society. This is not inconsistent with the focus of Critical Social Justice on social harmony, except that, as we will see, Stoicism places primary responsibility on the individual to cultivate reason as a way of assessing the world around him as he makes his way on the path to virtue, whereas Critical Social Justice is dubious about reason as a consistently reliable means of generating an adequate critique of existing institutions and achieving social harmony.[75]

The Stoics believed that decision-making and the circumstances in which decisions are made are co-determined. Thus, while the Stoics emphasized human agency, they did so with an understanding of our place in the universe as deterministic. This is not the place to delve deeply into Stoic physics, but this difference can perhaps best be illustrated by an example offered by the early Stoic philosopher Chrysippus. Kai Whiting and Leonidas Konstantakos, authors of *Being Better: Stoicism for a World Worth Living In*, provide a nice summary of Chrysippus's argument by analogy:

> Chrysippus argued that our actions and decisions are like a cylinder, which does not roll merely because it can. While its cylindrical form makes a rolling motion possible, that does not mean it *will* roll. For that to happen it must be placed on a sloped surface or pushed. Thus, the combination of the cylinder's shape, which makes it conducive to rolling, and external factors, such as a sloped environment, cause it to move. The cylinder represents our character; the slope or push represents our circumstances.[76]

In short, in the parlance of modern philosophy, the Stoics were compatibilists—they understood free will and determinism as compatible rather than incompatible with each other. As Massimo Pigliucci and others note, the Stoics highlighted the central role of *prohairesis*, our will or "principal cause" according to Cicero (generally recognized not as a Stoic but as an authority on the principles of Stoic philosophy), as one of the many causes of action in the universe.[77] These ideas of the ancient Stoics have long outlasted the authorities with which they came into conflict in their lives. They are still relevant today and offer an alternative way to think about social justice.

This alternative revolves around an understanding of virtue. Canceling has become a kind of virtue *signaling*, a way of enforcing orthodox ideas about virtue when heterodox ideas are "triggering." There is clearly disagreement about what constitutes virtue. There is overlap in how Stoicism and social justice activism think about virtue but there is the critical difference that Stoicism places responsibility for virtue in the individual and his inborn ability to cultivate an excellent character, while social justice activism places responsibility in institutions, or what the Stoics call "externals," with individuals being malleable vessels through whom institutional "virtue" is enacted.

Cancel culture highlights an important difference that arises between Stoicism and social justice activism. To the extent we encourage the *signaling* of virtue, we do not necessarily encourage virtue itself. For the Stoics, virtue is enough. Signaling virtue potentially makes you believe your well-being depends on whether other people recognize your virtue. In other words, your virtue depends on the opinions of others rather than the rational assessment of yourself by your reasoning faculty. Focusing instead on virtue alone, regardless of whether other people notice it, places the responsibility on individuals to cultivate reason and work toward developing a character geared toward justice, as well as the three other cardinal virtues of wisdom, temperance, and courage.

When Tom Cruise recently gave back his three Golden Globe awards to protest a lack of diversity on the body in charge,[78] did he do so because he was virtuous or because he wanted to signal virtue that he did not actually have? We cannot speak for Mr. Cruise. We only ask the question to highlight the distinction. For the Stoics, virtue is rooted in moral intent and good character. Given their conception of human nature, and nature more broadly, the Stoics see virtue as rooted in excellence of character, cultivated through reason. If Tom Cruise is virtuous, he acted because he believes as a matter of rational judgment that increasing diversity is a good cause. Since he sacrificed well-earned awards, there is good reason to give him the benefit of the doubt.

As creatures endowed by nature with reason, which allows us to recognize what is good, we are virtuous only if we pursue virtue for its own sake, not for the benefit that may accrue from it. Virtue-signaling hints at the pursuit of virtue for the reputation one obtains from the opinions of other people to whom we signal our virtue. Otherwise, why would we signal our virtue?

For the Stoics, there is no need to signal virtue because the well-lived life (*eudaimonia*) does not depend on the opinions of others. One consideration, however, is that publicizing virtue as Cruise did may be intended to bring attention to a lack of diversity, in which case Cruise's action was a matter of virtue in the interest of justice rather than virtue-signaling in the interest of his brand. In any case, our obligation is to be virtuous, regardless of whether people notice it. When we are, we come closer to a state of *eudaimonia*, a state in which we are content because our reason follows the dictates of nature, not the sound and fury of "externals" that trigger us.

Both Stoicism and social justice activism encourage us to be better people. The difference is that Stoicism starts with individuals as the basis for improving the community,[79] while social justice ideology starts with institutions as the basis for helping, even reforming, individuals. They overlap in recognizing that we all must be agents for change, but they diverge in where they locate the place in which virtue fundamentally resides. From this starting point, we will discover other points of divergence.

For example, the Stoics posit a naturalistic conception of reality in which reason is at the forefront of human thought and action. This view is rooted in the Stoic conception of reason as a distinguishing feature of humanity, an endowment from nature designed to pursue the cultivation of truth and good moral character. "The raw material of the good man," Epictetus claimed, "is his mind—his goal being to respond to impressions the way nature intended. As a general rule, nature designed the mind to assent to what is true, dissent from what is false and suspend judgment in doubtful cases" (*Discourses*, Book III, 3, 1–2).

"Similarly," Epictetus continues, nature "conditioned the mind to desire what is good, to reject what is bad and to regard with indifference what is neither one nor the other" (*Discourses*, Book III, 3, 2). Meanwhile, social justice scholarship and activism tend to view human nature as culturally malleable and take a historicist view of social reality that is suspicious of reason as a consistently reliable starting point for human thought and action.

This divergence reveals differences of perspective on a variety of issues related to social justice concerns, such as the nature and consequences of so-called "microaggressions" (explored in the next chapter), the nature and consequences of "toxic" or "traditional" masculinity (see discussion of the APA guidelines above and below), and the nature and consequences of "whiteness" in relation to racial inequality (explored in chapter 4). One might be inclined to believe that, for the Stoics, the ego is more important than social obligations because one must tend to one's own character, while for the Critical Social Justice advocate, one must tend to the character of the institutions in which we are embedded like "fish in the sea" (to use an analogy sometimes invoked in the Critical Social Justice literature).

This would be a mistake. "If," Epictetus clarified, "we locate the good in soundness of character, then it becomes good to maintain these relationships" (*Discourses*, Book III, 3, 8). In other words, just as free will and determinism are compatible in the Stoic worldview, tending to one's own character is compatible with, and even an important condition of, or inseparable from, tending to the character of social institutions. The resolution, as we will see in subsequent chapters, lies in an understanding of virtue.

(UPPERCASE) STOICISM, NOT (LOWERCASE) STOICISM

A tendency to believe that social conditions can pervert the use of reason, and a strain of skepticism about objectivity, are prevalent in the world of social justice commentary, which perhaps helps to explain why the ideas, beliefs, narratives, sensibilities, and reflexes that have become associated with social justice activism are susceptible to cognitive errors in reasoning, or histrionic overreactions to nuanced realities. Examples of erroneous reasoning are confirmation bias (the tendency to believe what you want to believe, ignoring contradictory evidence) and availability bias (the tendency, for example, to believe that headline news events are more common than they are).

This gives rise to a wider concern that the social justice movement's otherwise-appropriate concerns about oppression and marginalization in society have become "reified"—a favorite term of the Frankfurt School. This means that abstract ideas like "toxic masculinity" or "traditional masculinity" are treated as rigid, concrete realities—anthropomorphically exerting their influence through the way we live. They are so embedded in the intellectual and emotional reflexes of activists that they have ceased to be flexible concepts that usefully guide our investigation and interpretation of events and circumstances in society. They have become more like preexisting narratives into which the situational intricacies of lived experience are shoehorned.

The result is that notions like "toxic masculinity" or "traditional masculinity" become so overused and fetishized as heuristics that they lose their meaning; yet they continue to exert an outsized effect on how we understand reality and how we interact with it. When ideas like "toxic masculinity" are relentlessly and reflexively applied to situations where they may not apply, we gradually acquire not only an oversimplified view of reality, but also a distorted view, like how Hollywood glamorizes a narrative at the expense of marginalized, peripheral, or otherwise distinct narratives. They function as ideology rather than insight, obscuring the granularities of experience and obstructing a dynamic evaluation of the intricacies of unique situations on their own merits.

For example, a man who takes a Stoic approach to life, resulting in an authentic relationship with the emotional currents within him, may instead be perceived as being prone to an unhealthy degree of emotional repression, simply because he views emotional restraint, which is not the same as emotional repression, as an optimal approach to the management of one's spontaneous emotions.

Stoicism is thus misconstrued as a mere "power-through" stopgap, a repression of emotions to get through times of extreme duress, as might be the case in war—rather than a mature cultivation of philosophical perspectives on themes like mortality, suffering, and misfortune.[80] Stoicism, or rather, a layman misconception about Stoicism, is perceived as a tactical means of "getting by" before ultimately coming to terms with one's emotions, rather than a strategic acclimation to the perturbations of human existence. In short, we lose the distinction between "lowercase" stoicism and "uppercase" Stoicism.

To pigeonhole Stoicism into this preexisting narrative, then, is to misconstrue what Stoicism is about (and perhaps deprive men of a healthy coping strategy). The whole point of Stoicism is to recognize feelings as rooted in the natural order of the universe, as unavoidable as other aspects of life. The question then becomes how to acclimate to the vulnerabilities to which feelings give voice, rather than to avoid these feelings (and thus one's vulnerabilities) altogether. Social constructs are undoubtedly important and worthy of study, but they may not be the whole, or even a significant, reason why men may be reluctant to confront their underlying vulnerabilities. We might suggest instead that men have had an insufficient exposure to Stoic philosophy!

VIRTUE DEPENDS ON YOU

Stoicism can help not only men, but everyone, discover the power of reason as a path to *eudaimonia*. Reason, as an endowment from nature, brings us into harmony with nature. It does this by helping us cultivate virtue, the idea that character and moral intention mean more than the outcome of one's intentions. In other words, the journey is more important than the destination. Why? Because the journey is under your control. The destination is not. But you can help yourself along by doing the things that, as Professor Sellars notes, will consistently benefit you. These are the virtues of wisdom, justice, courage, and moderation—features of character that reason recognizes as being the basis for making positive contributions to the human community, and thus to oneself.

Another way of saying this is that Stoics encourage the use of "objective" reason to assess the intrinsic value of the virtues one embraces as the basis of character. Instrumental reason seeks the best means to attain one's ends on the presumption that the ends will bring happiness. Objective reason seeks to assess the intrinsic value of the ends to see if they are worth pursuing. As creatures of reason, we are personally responsible for identifying these ends—figuring out the nature of who we are and what ends to pursue to live in accord with who we are. Individual autonomy and agency are key. Happiness is about aligning good character with good ends, without getting out of sorts about whether we obtain these ends because they are outside our control.

In contrast to the Frankfurt School, the Stoics seem to have been inclined to view Odysseus as the kind of man to use "objective" reason to assess the intrinsic value of the virtues as the basis of character. In chapter 5, we will encounter the notion of the "Stoic sage" as a unicorn-like person who manages to arrive at a state of Stoic perfection—that is, the wise man who makes all the right moral decisions purely as a matter of habit and character. The Stoic sage was viewed as a "first class" character that "springs into existence . . . only once in five hundred years,"[81]

Seneca and Plutarch, however, suggested Odysseus as a model for the Stoic sage for actions such as "bravely entering Troy in rags" and "resisting both Calypso and Circe." Odysseus did not perpetuate injustice by reclaiming his throne in a world deemed unjust simply by a division between rulers and ruled. Instead, Odysseus rid Ithaca of the riotous suitors and restored his virtuous reign.

As it depended on Odysseus to rule Ithaca in a virtuous fashion, it depends on you to do your best to "exercise . . . what is in [your] power" (*Enchiridion*, XIV) and live virtuously. As explained in more detail in chapter 3, virtue arises from determining one's actions by reason such that they are in harmony with nature. An example might be seeking treatment when diagnosed with a serious illness, as self-preservation is the most basic of natural impulses in life forms; contributing to GoFundMe campaigns for cancer patients less financially fortunate than you are; making even greater effort to make sure you treat patients with a serious illness, and other disabled people, with respect and dignity; and to keep living your life to the fullest extent possible as long as you can.

It should not be unreasonable to presume that Stoicism and Critical Social Justice can agree on these terms. But Critical Theory underpins a social justice movement that is trying to convince the world that, if we are to advance the cause of social justice, we need to seriously scrutinize notions like objectivity, the "rational autonomy" of liberal humanism, and universalism. Stoicism, however, insists that virtue—underpinned by reason, objectivity, and a cosmopolitan view of humanity and its place in the world—can be of great service in the quest for social justice.

NOTES

1. Diogenes Laertius, *Lives of the Eminent Philosophers*, p. 228.

2. Massimo Pigliucci, "Free Speech and Virtue Ethics," *Areo Magazine*, May 20, 2021.

3. Pierre Hadot, *The Inner Citadel: The Meditations of Marcus Aurelius* (Cambridge, London: Harvard University Press, 1998), p. 61.

4. Max Horkheimer and Theodor W. Adorno, *Dialectic of Enlightenment* (New York: Continuum, 1998). Herbert Marcuse, *Eros and Civilization: A Philosophical Inquiry into Freud* (Boston: Beacon Press, 1955, 1966, 1974).

5. Max Horkheimer and Theodor W. Adorno, *Dialectic of Enlightenment*, p. 122.

6. Curtis Bowman, "Odysseus and the Siren Call of Reason: The Frankfurt School Critique of Enlightenment," *Other Voices, The (e) Journal of Cultural Criticism*, vol. 1 no. 1, March 1997.

7. Roland G. Fryer Jr., "An Empirical Analysis of Racial Differences in Police Use of Force," NBER Working Paper 22399, July 2016, Revised January 2018.

8. George A. Akerlof and Rachel E. Kranton, *Identity Economics: How Our Identities Shape Our Work, Wages, and Well-Being*, Princeton University

Press, 2010, https://press.princeton.edu/books/paperback/9780691152554/identity-economics.

9. How to Be a Stoic: John Sellars in Conversation with Donald J. Robertson (16:30): https://www.youtube.com/watch?v=ltFgRz-jhII.

10. Pierre Hadot, *The Inner Citadel*, pp. 154–155.

11. John Sellars, Aligning with Your Nature, Finding Meaning & the Stoic Approach to Emotions (10:30): https://www.youtube.com/watch?v=dLZheK7ygIg.

12. Pierre Hadot, *The Inner Citadel*, p. 75.

13. Pierre Hadot, *The Inner Citadel*, pp. 76–77.

14. Julia Annas, *Intelligent Virtue*, p. 105.

15. Pierre Hadot, *The Inner Citadel*, p. 77.

16. Stoicism, *Stanford Encyclopedia of Philosophy*, first published Monday April 15, 1996; substantive revision Tuesday April 10, 2018, https://plato.stanford.edu/entries/stoicism/.

17. Stoicism, *Stanford Encyclopedia of Philosophy*, first published Monday April 15, 1996; substantive revision Tuesday April 10, 2018, https://plato.stanford.edu/entries/stoicism/.

18. Julia Annas, *Intelligent Virtue*, p. 150.

19. Julia Annas, *Intelligent Virtue*, p. 152.

20. Michael Sugrue, Marcus Aurelius: Lecture on Stoicism (35:20): https://www.youtube.com/watch?v=L5_an6B3H4E.

21. Pierre Hadot, *The Inner Citadel*, p. 213.

22. It should be noted that this is the opposite conclusion suggested by Kant in his paper "On a Supposed Right to Lie from Philanthropic Concerns." Kant, Immanuel, "On a Supposed Right to Tell Lies from Benevolent Motives," In: T. K. Abbott (trans.), *Kant's Critique of Practical Reason and Other Works on the Theory of Ethics* (London: Longmans, Green and Co., 1898). See also, https://en.wikipedia.org/wiki/On_a_Supposed_Right_to_Tell_Lies_from_Benevolent_Motives.

23. Korsgaard, Christine, "The Right to Lie: Kant on Dealing with Evil," *Philosophy and Public Affairs* (1986) 15, No. 4, pp. 325–349.

24. Pierre Hadot, *The Inner Citadel*, p. 217.

25. Pierre Hadot, *The Inner Citadel*, p. 215.

26. Pierre Hadot, *The Inner Citadel*, p. 215.

27. Stoicism, *Stanford Encyclopedia of Philosophy*, first published Monday April 15, 1996; substantive revision Tuesday April 10, 2018, https://plato.stanford.edu/entries/stoicism/.

28. Pierre Hadot, *The Inner Citadel*, pp. 83–84.

29. Julia Annas, *Intelligent Virtue*, p. 161.

30. Julia Annas, *Intelligent Virtue*, p. 75.

31. Julia Annas, *Intelligent Virtue*, p. 82.

32. Pierre Hadot, *The Inner Citadel*, p. 75.

33. Max Horkheimer, *Eclipse of Reason*, pp. 5, 7.

34. Emily Wilson, *Seneca: A Life* (Penguin, 2016), p. 15.

35. Emily Wilson, *Seneca: A Life*, p. 14.

36. Emily Wilson, *Seneca: A Life*, p. 15.

37. Pierre Hadot, *The Inner Citadel*, p. 74.

38. Emily Wilson, *Seneca: A Life*, p. 15.

39. Gary Becker, "The Economic Approach to Human Behavior," in *The Economic Approach to Human Behavior* (Chicago and London: The University of Chicago Press, 1976), p. 5.

40. Donald Robertson, *How to Think Like a Roman Emperor*, p. 137.

41. Stephanie Pappas, "APA Issues First-Ever Guidelines for Practice with Men and Boys," *American Psychological Association*, 2019, vol. 50, no. 1.

42. "APA Guidelines for Psychological Practice with Boys and Men," August 2018, p. 2.

43. "APA Guidelines for Psychological Practice with Boys and Men," August 2018, p. 6.

44. Stephanie Pappas, "APA Issues First-Ever Guidelines for Practice with Men and Boys," *American Psychological Association*, 2019, vol. 50, no. 1.

45. Jonathan Church, "Stoic, Toxic, or More Confusion?," the Good Men Project February 16, 2019, https://goodmenproject.com/ethics-values/stoic-toxic-or-more-confusion-wcz/.

46. Tony Long, "Stoicism Ancient and Modern," Stoicon 2018, 30:30, https://www.youtube.com/watch?v=_xuQ4i46K_M&t=7s.

47. Anthony Long on Epictetus and Socrates (48:20): https://www.youtube.com/watch?v=HzZyT_kHl84

48. Max Horkheimer, *Critical Theory: Selected Essays* (New York: Continuum, 1999), p. 208.

49. Özlem Sensoy and Robin DiAngelo, *Is Everyone Really Equal?*, p. 4.

50. Max Horkheimer, *Critical Theory: Selected Essays*, p. 222.

51. Özlem Sensoy and Robin DiAngelo, *Is Everyone Really Equal?*, p. 4.

52. Helen Pluckrose, "What Do We Mean by Critical Social Justice?," Counterweight, February 17, 2021, https://counterweightsupport.com/2021/02/17/what-do-we-mean-by-critical-social-justice/.

53. M. A. Rafey Habib, "The Myth of Liberal Humanim," Rutgers University, 2021, https://habib.camden.rutgers.edu/publications/essays/the-myth-of-liberal-humanism/.

54. Richard Delgado and Jean Stefancic, *Critical Race Theory: An Introduction* (New York: New York University Press, 2017), p. 3.

55. Richard Delgado and Jean Stefancic, *Critical Race Theory: The Cutting Edge* (Philadelphia: Temple University Press, 2013), p. 3.

56. Richard Delgado and Jean Stefancic, *Critical Race Theory: The Cutting Edge*, p. 3.

57. Kai Whiting and Leonidas Konstantakos, *Being Better*, p. 1.

58. Pierre Hadot, *The Inner Citadel*, pp. 101–105.

59. René Brouwer, *The Stoic Sage: The Early Stoics on Wisdom, Sagehood, and Socrates* (Cambridge, New York, Melbourne, New Delhi: Cambridge University Press, 2014), p. 118.

60. John Sellars | Aligning with Your Nature, Finding Meaning & the Stoic Approach to Emotions (35:45), https://www.youtube.com/watch?v=dLZheK7yglg

61. Margaret R. Graver, *Stoicism and Emotion* (Chicago and London: The University of Chicago Press, 2007), p. 5.

62. Baruch Spinoza, *The Ethics* (Indianapolis: Hackett Publishing Company, 1982), p. 175.

63. "Malaria No More Applauds The U.S. President's Malaria Initiative on 15 Years of Transformative Impact," Malaria No More, June 29, 2020, https://www.malarianomore.org/news/malaria-no-more-applauds-the-u-s-presidents-malaria-initiative-on-15-years-of-transformative-impact/.

64. Helen Tilley, PhD, "Medicine, Empires, and Ethics in Colonial Africa," *AMA Journal of Ethics*, 2016, 18(7), 743–753.

65. Helen Tilley, PhD, "Medicine, Empires, and Ethics in Colonial Africa," *AMA Journal of Ethics*, 2016, 18(7), 743–753.

66. Peter Boghossian and James Lindsay, *How to Have Impossible Conversations: A Very Practical Guide* (New York: Lifelong Books, 2019).

67. Peter Boghossian, "My University Sacrificed Ideas for Ideology. So Today I Quit," September 8, 2021, https://bariweiss.substack.com/p/my-university-sacrificed-ideas-for.

68. "A Letter on Justice and Open Debate," *Harper's Magazine*, July 7, 2020, https://harpers.org/a-letter-on-justice-and-open-debate/.

69. Conor Friedersdorf, "The Chilling Effect of an Attack on a Scholar?", *The Atlantic*, July 20, 2020.

70. Conor Friedersdorf, "The Chilling Effect of an Attack on a Scholar?", *The Atlantic*, July 20, 2020.

71. Jessie Tu, "Journalist, Emily Wilder sacked by AP over allegedly biased Facebook post," *Women's Agenda*, May 24, 2021.

72. M. A. Rafey Habib, "The Myth of Liberal Humanim," Rutgers University, 2021, https://habib.camden.rutgers.edu/publications/essays/the-myth-of-liberal-humanism/.

73. How to Be a Stoic: John Sellars in Conversation with Donald Robertson (56:15): https://www.youtube.com/watch?v=ltFgRz-jhII

74. This is a point on which people can disagree. See, for example, Charles Mills, *The Racial Contract* (Ithaca, London: Cornell University Press, 1997), p. 129.

75. Kai Whiting and Leonidas Konstantakos, *Being Better*, p. 54.

76. Anthony Long on Epictetus and Socrates (46:50, 48:15): https://www.youtube.com/watch?v=HzZyT_kHl84

77. "Golden Globes Crisis: Tom Cruise Returns Awards and NBC Drops Ceremony," *BBC News*, May 11, 2021.

78. How to Be a Stoic: John Sellars in Conversation with Donald Robertson (49:30), https://www.youtube.com/watch?v=ltFgRz-jhII.

79. Stephanie Pappas, "APA Issues First-Ever Guidelines for Practice with Men and Boys," *American Psychological Association*, 2019, vol. 50, no. 1.

80. Lucius Seneca, *Letters from a Stoic*, Letter 42, p. 167.

81. René Brouwer, *The Stoic Sage*, p. 111.

Chapter 2

Social Justice Activism in the Twenty-First Century

In *The Coddling of the American Mind*, Jonathan Haidt and Greg Lukianoff note an upsurge in a certain strain of student activism on college campuses. In 2013, Lukianoff "began hearing about students asking for 'triggering' material to be removed from courses."[1] *The New York Times* and *The New Republic* published reports on the same topic in the spring of 2014.[2]

In 2015, almost twenty years after film critic David Denby defended Columbia University's traditional core curriculum in *Great Books*,[3] "four Columbia undergraduates wrote an essay in the school newspaper arguing that students 'need to feel safe in the classroom' but 'many texts in the Western canon' are 'wrought with histories and narratives of exclusion and oppression' and contain 'triggering and offensive material that marginalizes student identities in the classroom.'" Students worried that texts in the Western canon contained content that could be harmful to their mental health.[4]

In contrast to past generations of student activism, Haidt and Lukianoff claim, student activism in the 2010s was unique in its apprehension over psychological "fragility." Students seemed to fear they would suffer irreparable mental and emotional anguish from encounters with "triggering" material in canonical texts. Haidt and Lukianoff describe this presumption as the Untruth of Fragility: *What doesn't kill you makes you weaker.*[5] This was a matter of concern to Lukianoff because he believed "many university students are learning to think in distorted ways," which "increases their likelihood of becoming fragile, anxious, and easily hurt."[6] He wanted to get to the bottom of it.

Lukianoff had a theory: "Students were beginning to demand protection from speech because they had unwittingly learned to employ the very cognitive distortions that CBT [cognitive-behavioral therapy] tries to correct." Lukianoff and Haidt subsequently met to discuss Haidt's research on "the power of CBT and its close fit with ancient wisdom."[7] Their collaboration led to an article in *The Atlantic,* "The Coddling of the American Mind," and then a book with the same title.

Their basic thesis was "that many parents, K–12 teachers, professors, and university administrators have been unknowingly teaching a generation of students to engage in the mental habits commonly seen in people who suffer from anxiety and depression."[8] Their book goes on to elaborate on their thesis and document a body of evidence to support it. One point, which arises only briefly in their book, involves a reference to Stoicism in relation to "the power of CBT and its close fit with ancient wisdom."[9]

This is a point that has gained attention in recent years. Psychotherapist Donald Robertson, for example, has authored a book on the Stoic roots of cognitive-behavioral therapy.[10] He has also written elsewhere on the Stoic underpinnings of CBT in articles and interviews.[11] Massimo Pigliucci, author of *How to Be a Stoic* and professor of philosophy at the City College of New York, also makes the connection.[12]

The ancient Greek and Roman philosophy of Stoicism offers sound advice on how one might handle "triggering" material. As an example, note that it is virtually certain you will be insulted by someone at some point in life. The Stoics had something to say about this. Haidt and Lukianoff make note of it in a section of their book on "why it is such a bad idea to tell students that words are violence."[13] Arguing that words can be considered violence only if one chooses to interpret them as violence—that is, interpret the words to have a meaning that increases psychic stress—they quote the ancient Roman Emperor and Stoic philosopher Marcus Aurelius: "Choose not to be harmed—and you won't feel harmed. Don't feel harmed—and you haven't been."[14]

Haidt, Lukianoff, and Marcus Aurelius are implicitly invoking what Stoic writer William Irvine calls insult pacifism, the idea that "when insulted, we should not insult back in return," but "instead carry on as if nothing had happened."[15] When the insulter realizes he has failed "to provoke a rise in his target, an insulter is likely to feel foolish."[16] How can this be effective? As Epictetus, said: "Men are disturbed not by things, but by the views which they take of things" (*Enchiridion*, V). Further, "it is we who torment, we who make difficulties for ourselves—that is, our opinions do" (*Discourses*, Book I, 25, 28): Just consider a rock.

> Stand by a rock and insult it, and what have you accomplished? If someone responds to an insult like a rock, what has the abuser gained with his invective? If, however, he has his victim's weakness to exploit, then his efforts are worth his while (*Discourses*, Book I, 25, 29).

Of course, human beings are not rocks. Insults do not ricochet off our minds so easily. The aspersions cast by an offender can easily trigger spikes in stress that stem from physiological reactions. But these immediate spikes in stress are physical responses within us to physical stimuli impressed upon us from outside us. The harm arises when our "inner discourse" formulates a belief about the stimulus and our reason decides it is harmful. To state the matter as factually as a Stoic might recommend, the transmission of verbal sounds from the mouth of the person who utters the sounds to the eardrum of the person who receives the sound terminates in a value judgment by the person receiving the sound. The mind of the person interprets, or *judges*, the words as an insult, and then assents to this judgment.

This assent is a point of demarcation between the utterance of words and the "emotion" of feeling insulted. As already noted, Margaret Graver distinguishes between "felt sensations in themselves and felt sensations as produced by particular kinds of judgment."[17] In this sense, human beings are not like rocks.

However, it is when we describe the occurrence in physical terms—verbal sounds transmitted from the mouth of the person who utters the sounds to the eardrum of the person who hears the sound—that we see we are not entirely unlike rocks. As an objective matter, human beings and rocks are both physical objects on the receiving end of air vibrations caused by "insults." The difference only becomes apparent when we realize that "insult" involves a value judgment. Only a human being endowed with a faculty of judgment can translate air vibrations into insults.

This capacity for judgment implies that human beings decide what these air vibrations mean. As Massimo Pigliucci and Gregory Lopez write in *A Handbook for Stoics*:

> An insult is, in effect, a three-step process. First, someone has to say something to you that is meant to be offensive. Second, you have to take whatever has been said as offensive. Last, you have to react to the insult since, without a reaction, the insult falls flat. Eliciting your reaction is precisely what the other person wants. It is the very point of the insult.[18]

Do we let an insult, which reflects the opinion of an insulter, determine our sense of dignity and self-respect, or do we insist that our sense of dignity and self-respect depends on our own rational judgment? If the latter, as the Stoics would recommend by urging us to cultivate a virtuous character, the insult is the insulter's problem, not that of the insulted party. This Stoic advice lies behind modern cognitive-behavioral therapy. "The concept of radically *accepting* unpleasant feelings," writes therapist Donald Robertson, "has likewise become central to modern cognitive-behavioral therapy (CBT). Pain becomes *more painful* when we struggle against it, but the burden is often lightened, paradoxically, if we can accept the sensation and relax into it or even welcome it."[19]

A canonical text, often written by authors who lived in another era, is "triggering" only if you let it be. If, for example, you read *Gone with the Wind* anachronistically as a propaganda novel glorifying the Southern Confederacy (as prominent anti-racist activist and historian Ibram X. Kendi may be inclined to do given his critique of the film in *Stamped from the Beginning*),[20] rather than as a love story that humanizes Southerners while also exposing their racism and dehumanization of Black slaves, you may be "triggered." If you read the novel as a literary endeavor, partaking in a captivating story about life in the Southern Confederacy during the American Civil War, you have an opportunity to partake in the reading of great literature while improving your understanding of racial injustice.

For the Stoic, *Gone with the Wind* is an "external." You have no control over its contents and how it was written. You do have control over how to read and interpret it. You can choose to read it politically as a hagiographic romance novel eulogizing the "Lost Cause" of the Confederacy; or you can read it as a love story that simultaneously humanizes the people of the antebellum South while shining a bright light on their hypocrisy, hubris, and dehumanization of Black slaves.

If you decide upon the latter, you can have an enriching experience. You get to enjoy the literary quality of the work while getting a stark look not only at the insufferably self-centered Scarlett O'Hara, but at the horrid injustice of an antebellum society that allows the Tarleton twins to be "given" their Black childhood playmate Jeems "for their own on their tenth birthday."[21]

This is not the perspective many students have taken as universities witness an upsurge in "fragility" activism. Students seem more likely to view the depiction of antebellum society in *Gone with the Wind* as psychologically harmful with no compensatory value in terms of gaining insight into antebellum society's foundational injustice. They take the same approach to controversial speakers on campus.

Haidt and Lukianoff acknowledge that the notion of words as violence arose in the context of protesting controversial speakers coming to campus. One consequence of these protests, however, may be to raise the profile of those speakers. If these speakers did, in fact, intend to provoke students, they were successful. It is conceivable that if students chose instead to calmly engage in robust and rigorous critique of the ideas of speakers to whom they objected, the speakers would have a much harder time of it, possibly seeing their ideas delegitimized and their public profile diminished.

"Catastrophizing"—a term increasingly employed in public discourse, and which refers to the tendency to exaggerate or obsess over the threats of a situation—makes things worse. Rather than "de-platforming" controversial speakers, it can raise their profile, fueling more protest, anger, and anxiety over the ongoing public influence exerted by public figures to whom students objected.

Catastrophizing can also result in an increase, rather than decrease, in the psychological harm from which students claim to suffer. As Donald Robertson writes: "People who strongly believe that unpleasant feelings are bad and try to suppress them from their minds often become more tense and preoccupied with the very feelings they're trying to avoid, trapping themselves in a vicious cycle."[22] It might be worthwhile to consider the alternative approaches of dialogue or debate.

Of course, as not every Twitter thread is worth getting sucked into, we should not expect students to do the exhaustive work of arguing against every conceivable idea of every conceivable speaker invited to campuses. This is where wisdom, one of the four Stoic virtues, comes in.

The Stoics encourage us to cultivate reason in pursuit of wisdom. It is wisdom that facilitates our ability not only to engage in dialogue or debate, but to recognize when it is worth doing so, as opposed to simply ignoring the superficial provocations of someone like Milo Yiannopoulos, the far-right provocateur and former Breitbart News editor known for his antagonistic stances against feminism, political correctness, and other causes dear to social justice activists.

Haidt and Lukianoff are concerned that when parents, K–12 teachers, professors, and university administrators enable "fragility" activism, they are not helping, but harming, students by failing to help them develop the resilience they will need to confront and overcome the many challenges life will inevitably present.

Why?

As the Stoics might suggest, the "fragility" mindset anchors our mental health, and our ability to cope with adversity, on "externals" such as canonical texts, insults, and innumerable other aspects of our environment, rather than on our own internal capacity to not worry about what we cannot control and respond instead to what we can control. For instance, we can acknowledge that canonical texts were written from perspectives that do not always align with current values, without feeling as if errant perspectives are directly aimed at us.

In the *Fragments*, Epictetus is recorded as saying: "People with a strong constitution can tolerate extremes of hot and cold; people of strong mental health can handle anger, grief, joy and the other emotions" (*Fragments*, 20). Taking this view, we can accomplish two things: (1) we can appreciate and learn from the literary quality of the work as constructed, while (2) also engaging in critique of the perspectives that, while outdated, may help us learn about oppression in the past and how it may still prevail in the present.

MICROAGGRESSIONS AND SOCIAL JUSTICE ACTIVISM

Stoicism is not the recipe student activism has employed in the 2010s (and now 2020s). One manifestation is the widespread adoption of the term "microaggression," a term first coined by Harvard psychiatrist Chester Pierce in the 1970s. It was anointed the top word of 2015 by the Global Language Monitor, eight years after publication of a paper by Derald Wing Sue and colleagues that popularized the term by drawing a connection between alleged microaggressions and psychological harm.

Defining microaggressions as "brief and commonplace daily verbal, behavioral, or environmental indignities, whether intentional or unintentional, that communicate hostile, derogatory, or negative racial slights and insults toward people of color,"[23] the paper spawned a wave of academic research and elevated the term into the mainstream conversation about race and discrimination. "Trigger warnings" and "safe spaces" on university campuses are conspicuous legacies of this paper.

Let's review a few examples. In 2015, a group identifying itself as Black Students at Emory University called for undergraduate course evaluations to include two "open-ended questions" asking students whether professors have "made any micro-aggressions towards you on account of your race, ethnicity, gender, sexual orientation, language, and/or other identity," which they believed "would help to ensure that there are repercussions or sanctions for racist actions performed by professors."[24]

At Occidental College, faculty voted on implementation of a policy to allow students to report professors who commit microaggressions.[25] The Inclusive Excellence Center at the University of Wisconsin-Milwaukee designated "politically correct" as a microaggression because it purportedly dismisses concerns about speech insensitivities.[26] Corporate workplaces have also incorporated microaggression awareness into diversity-training programs. The medical profession as well.

The microaggression paradigm is a vivid manifestation of how, in the years immediately preceding and following publication of Haidt and Lukianoff's *Atlantic* article, student activism merged with a powerful wave of social justice activism that was erupting in the broader society. Motivated by well-intentioned and well-founded concerns about the disempowered status of historically marginalized social groups, movements like Black Lives Matter and #MeToo were generating media attention on issues like police brutality, sexual harassment, and sexual assault.

Black Lives Matter emerged while waves of mass protests erupted over the killings of Michael Brown, Walter Scott, Freddie Gray, Eric Garner, and others. In 2017, the #MeToo movement exploded with countless stories of the sexual harassment and sexual assault of women by powerful men like Harvey Weinstein. There was also broad awareness of ongoing income and wealth inequality, which persisted in the wake of the Occupy Wall Street and Tea Party populist outbursts following the financial crisis.

It all reached a crescendo in 2020, when video captured Minneapolis police officer Derek Chauvin with his knee on the neck of a handcuffed George Floyd, who pleaded "I can't breathe" before dying. As a pandemic raged around the world, protesters throughout the United States amassed in dense urban areas to express their demands for justice.

Meanwhile, in 2016, Donald Trump was elected president of the United States. In the same year, Jordan Peterson came to fame. Trump was a provocateur who relied on his fame, fortune, and charismatic, if crude, rhetorical style to ride a wave of populist discontent on the reactionary Right. Peterson, however, was a well-respected academic psychologist who was among the first prominent figures to publicly criticize academia as a source of ideas underlying an intellectual framework that, he claimed, was driving a virulent strain of intolerance in the name of social justice.

When social justice activism burst out into the open in the 2010s, events found ideas ready-made for providing a theoretical, and ideological, lens through which social justice concerns could be filtered.

A HISTORICAL PRIMER ON CRITICAL SOCIAL JUSTICE

Social justice scholarship and activism in the 2010s, and now 2020s, rely on a specific way of understanding social justice—specifically, what Robin DiAngelo and Özlem Sensoy call *Critical* Social Justice. In *Is Everyone Really Equal? An Introduction to Key Concepts in Social Justice Education*, Sensoy and DiAngelo explain that a "critical approach to social justice refers to specific theoretical perspectives that recognize that society is *stratified* (i.e., divided and unequal) in significant and far-reaching ways along social group lines that include race, class, gender, sexuality, and ability." This definition "is rooted in a critical theoretical approach" that "refers to a broad range of fields" and "recognizes inequality as deeply embedded in the fabric of society." Naturally, Critical Social Justice scholarship and activism "actively seeks to change this."[27]

Key tenets of Critical Social Justice are that people are not just individuals, but members of social groups, and that these groups "are valued unequally in society." Critical Social Justice works to undo institutional arrangements that allocate more of society's resources to social groups valued more highly by society than to social groups seen as having less value to society. It is committed to a "lifelong process" of "self-reflection" on how people are socialized into their groups in ways that perpetuate these structural inequalities. It encourages people to cultivate an awareness of their group membership ("positionality") and to act "in ways that challenge social injustice."[28] The idea is to think "critically" about social position, social relations, and the "knowledge" that underpins it all.[29]

This seemingly innocuous paradigm emerges from a historical convergence in the twentieth century between social movements in the 1960s and 1970s and scholarship within a set of academic fields that gave intellectual shape to the aspirations of these movements. That is, social justice scholarship gave voice to social justice activism. The field that puts it all together is Critical Theory.

DiAngelo and Sensoy describe Critical Theory as "a specific scholarly approach that explores the historical, cultural, and ideological lines of authority that underlie social conditions."[30] Developed in the first half of the twentieth century by the Frankfurt School (as we have already explored in the previous chapter), the Critical Theory of Max Horkheimer and others "developed in part as a response to [the] presumed superiority and infallibility of scientific method, and raised questions about whose rationality and whose presumed objectivity underlies scientific methods."[31]

In other words, when it comes to knowledge and justice, the question is not whether the use of our reason leads to objective knowledge about what is just, or, as the ancient Stoic philosophers might say, to a "secure cognition"[32] of reality that then leads to rational choices and actions in harmony with the world, or Logos. It is about power, or: "who benefits from that knowledge claim and whose lives are limited by it?"[33]

The work of "continental" philosophers who "were also grappling with similar questions" about power and knowledge and justice, such as Jacques Derrida, Michel Foucault, Pierre Bourdieu, and Jacques Lacan, then "merges in the North American context of the 1960s with antiwar, feminist, gay rights, Black power, Indigenous Peoples and other emerging social justice movements."[34]

This is not a story told only by DiAngelo and Sensoy. Professors Douglas Kellner and Tyson Lewis (of the University of California, Los Angeles and the University of North Texas, respectively) tell a similar story in a thoughtful overview of liberal humanism and the European critical tradition. Tracing

Critical Theory back to the philosophy of Immanuel Kant, Kellner and Lewis explain that,

> for Kant, critique consisted of tracing the origins of experience back to the faculties of the mind. Stated simply, before Kant, science described the world passively, but after Kant, science was seen to write onto the world what human categories imposed upon it. For Kantians, science no longer extracted knowledge from the proverbial thing-in-itself (which remains fundamentally unknowable): rather science produced knowledge of the phenomena of the world.[35]

Similarly, Professor Matthew McManus traces Critical Theory back to Kant in writing: "The idea of a critique, which looked not just to expose bad ideas but diagnose their roots in broader ideologies and practices, took off and began to have a profound influence. We saw everything from critiques of 'post-colonial reason' to 'the political economy of the sign' and even 'everyday life.'"[36]

Kellner and Lewis provide a highly informative overview of the history of ideas—covering the works of Georg Hegel, Karl Marx, Friedrich Nietzsche, Michel Foucault, Sigmund Freud, the Frankfurt School, and the Birmingham School—behind the development of Critical Theory and its modus operandi of locating ideas in the ideological milieu of their social, political, economic, and historical circumstances.

Kellner and Lewis end with the "poststructuralist moment of the late 1960s and 1970s," when "there was a proliferation of new critical theories that connected with new social movements, producing a proliferation of 'posts' and theory wars from the 1970s to the present." These critical theories, which included postcolonial studies, feminisms, critical race theory, queer theory, "and other groupings associated with new oppositional political movements," "turned to a 'politics of representation' during the 1960s and 1970s that linked critique with social movements."[37]

Cynical Theories, a 2020 book by Helen Pluckrose and James Lindsay, draws a similar road map in explaining how critical theories made everything about race, gender, and identity, and how this harms everybody.[38] Haidt and Lukianoff also invoke this history in tracing the emergence of the New Left to the influence of Herbert Marcuse—particularly his essay on "repressive tolerance,"[39] according to which revolutionary activism should discourage toleration of ideas germinating in the status quo. They note that Marcuse's "ideas were taken up by the generation of students in the 1960s and 1970s who are the older professors of today, so a Marcusean view is still widely available."[40]

In the ensuing decades, "oppositional political movements" petered out as the broader society grew weary with the extremism of activist groups such as Weatherman, the Symbionese Liberation Army, the United Freedom Front,

Sam Melville Jonathan Jackson unit, the FALN, and other groups, while the young activists of the 1960s like Bill Ayers, Michael Apple, Henry Giroux, Joe Kincheloe, Angela Davis, and others matured into social justice scholars as they retreated into universities during the Reagan Revolution.[41] Many of these scholars were influenced by Paulo Freire's *Pedagogy of the Oppressed* and Antonio Gramsci's neo-Marxism as they developed the field of Critical Pedagogy, which is Critical Theory as applied to philosophy and praxis of education.[42]

The fruits of their efforts began to take shape in the 1990s. This was right around the time when, according to Richardo Delgado and Jean Stefancic, critical race theory became a "self-conscious entity" and "began organizing in 1989, holding its first working session shortly thereafter."[43] In the introduction to their book *Critical Race Theory: An Introduction*, Delgado and Stefancic, who count "continental social and political philosophy" among the influences on critical race theory,[44] write that critical race theory "draws from certain European philosophers and theorists, such as Antonio Gramsci, Michel Foucault, and Jacques Derrida" (among other influences).[45]

Meanwhile, in a 1992 article, "The New Dark Age: The Frankfurt School and 'Political Correctness,'" Michael Minnicino describes the connection between the Frankfurt School and "political correctness," writing that "with the collapse of the Soviet Union, our campuses now represent the largest concentration of Marxist dogma in the world," even going so far as to complain that the "irrational adolescent outbursts of the 1960s have become institutionalized into a 'permanent revolution.'"[46]

Though Minnicino's article was published by "an organ of the Lyndon LaRouche movement *cum* cult" and became the basis for what many deem the antisemitic conspiracy theory of "cultural Marxism,"[47] it is true that the 1990s saw an outpouring of "culture war" controversies about campus speech codes, identity politics, multicultural education, political correctness, "great books" and "dead White males." Outside the university, Clinton's election in 1992 brought the Reagan-Bush years to an end, while the fall of the Soviet Union ended anti-communism as a unifying ideological theme patching together the disparate communities of the United States and the West. Meanwhile, the rise of Rush Limbaugh and the Gingrich Revolution of 1994 helped radicalize right-wing political forces in America.

Historically speaking, however, the evolution of social justice activism as it manifests today was still in its early chapters as the world celebrated the "end of history" while the regime of liberal democracy and global capitalism (and what many call "neoliberalism") celebrated its victory. Then 9/11 brought an end to America's "holiday from history."[48] The Iraq War channeled the energy of progressive activism into anti-war protest and resistance. The election of Barack Obama offered the Left a brief glimpse of "hope and change," but the financial crisis, Great Recession, Occupy Wall Street, and the Tea Party movement quickly brought "hope and change" back to earth.

By the time of Obama's reelection and the European debt crises of the early 2010s, disillusionment began to set in at a broad and deep level in Western societies. Cable news and talk radio, as well as digital spaces like social media, video streaming, YouTube, and the intellectual dark web have helped spread and amplify these concerns as well as the vehement polarization that has come along with them. Meanwhile, it is also worth noting that the ratio of professors who describe themselves as left-wing to professors who describe themselves as right-wing went from 2:1 in 1996 to 5:1 in 2011.[49]

The time was ripe for a new wave of progressive activism. It was around this time that Jonathan Haidt and Greg Lukianoff began noticing a new kind of activism among the Generation Z (a.k.a. iGen) students beginning to enter American universities. It is in this overall context that social justice activists and scholars in the early twenty-first century, following on the heels of developments in twentieth-century intellectual history and early twenty-first-century political and economic events, evinced a single-minded focus on systems of power as a perennial source of injustice in the world.

Whatever the discourse on justice, it seemed that all matters of conscience came down to an analysis of power relations, particularly the history of how groups in power have marshaled the resources of privilege at the expense of marginalized groups that have been excluded from power.

The twenty-first century social justice movement is galvanized by serious concerns about how power is used by dominant groups in society to exploit and oppress, enforced through socialized norms, attitudes, and behaviors that are usually invisible to the legions of powerful and powerless people who have not awakened from their ideological dormancy. In terms of academic scholarship, the focus is on how traditional theoretical development and analysis within various fields of scholarship unknowingly or unwittingly perpetuate systems of oppression by failing to connect their methodological and theoretical frameworks to the powerful social interests they reinforce.

As Max Horkheimer wrote in a 1937 essay, "the real social function of science is not made manifest" in traditional theory, which "speaks not of what theory means in human life, but only of what it means in the isolated sphere in which for historical reasons it comes into existence."[50]

The "scholar and his science are incorporated into the apparatus of society; his achievements are a factor in the conservation and continuous renewal of the existing state of affairs, no matter what fine names he gives to what he does."[51] Here we arrive at the core claim of Critical Theory: "The facts which our senses present to us are socially preformed in two ways: through the historical character of the object perceived and through the historical character of the perceiving organ."[52]

For Critical Theory, the "existence of society has either been founded directly on oppression or been the blind outcome of conflicting forces, but in any event not the result of conscious spontaneity on the part of free individuals."[53] Critical Theory, then, is intimately connected with the social justice activism of identity politics, particularly in the context of Western capitalism (as was the case for the Frankfurt School). As stated in the mid-1990s by the late Manning Marable, former professor of public affairs, history, and African American Studies at Columbia University:

> To be truly liberating, any social theory must reflect the actual problems of a historical conjuncture with a commitment to rigor and scholastic truth. . . . It must begin by critiquing the vast structure of power and privilege that characterizes the political economy of postindustrial, capitalist America.[54]

It should, of course, go without saying that the notion that justice should be concerned with dismantling cultures of exploitation and oppression that benefit some social groups at the expense of others is not problematic per se. It has, however, become so influential a paradigm that the social justice crusade risks instituting its own version of intellectual imperialism. When every inkling of concern about injustice is filtered through the lens of an overarching paradigm of social construction and historicized oppression, we might start to worry that the cause of social justice has been commandeered by a broad-based campaign of ideological obduracy that focuses obsessively on social and historical constructs as the sole legitimate concern for social justice.

There may be no concept more pertinent to this concern than intersectionality, according to which individuals are compositions of intersecting social identities such as race, gender, class, and sexual orientation. For example, one person may be a White, gay, disabled man, while another may be a Black, straight, able-bodied woman. Intersectional theory, which inspires much social justice scholarship and activism, is concerned with how these identities are constructed within social and historical circumstances and how they are related to institutional structures of domination and oppression.

Intersectionality posits that the sum is greater than the parts. For example, Kimberlé Crenshaw writes: "Because the intersectional experience is greater than the sum of racism and sexism, any analysis that does not take intersectionality into account cannot sufficiently address the particular manner in which Black women are subordinated."[55] A court may dismiss claims brought by Black women claiming a firm specifically discriminated against Black women as a class. If the firm hired White women for one type of job and Black men for another type of job, the court may decide that there is no valid claim because the firm's hiring policy did not discriminate by sex or race.[56]

This reasonable point has been transformed into a vital framework for a social justice movement for which the analysis of justice boils down to an analysis of social identity and social constructs. To repeat, social justice activism in the twenty-first century is all about identity politics. It is about all possible ways that people have been oppressed as a function of their social group identities. Despite differences in personal identity and experience, oppressed groups share the status of being a victim.

Intersectional solidarity takes precedence over sectarian loyalties if systems of power and privilege that unconscionably exploit their victims are to be confronted and overturned. As the late Manning Marable wrote in the context of race: "What is required is a radical break from the narrow, race-based politics of the past. . . . We must rethink and restructure the central social categories of collective struggle by which we conceive and understand our own political reality."[57]

In short, there is a relentless insistence on viewing the crucible of oppression endured by all victims of exploitation as rooted in entrenched historical developments that have their roots in a capitalist world order that has given rise to imperialism, cultural appropriation, Whiteness, heteronormative institutions, patriarchy, xenophobia, and other manifestations of oppression. The intersectional concerns of the social justice movement galvanize a culture of victimhood while advancing a worldview that subsumes all the complexities of justice under a foundational ideology of socially constructed oppression.

To reiterate, these are not unworthy concerns. It is not the nominal fight against structural oppression that raises qualms about the social justice crusade. It is, rather, the implication that a commitment to justice is equivalent to a commitment to revolution rather than reform, and that there is little or no value in prevailing norms, ideas, and institutions if they are not in some way connected to a concerted effort to overturn a status quo built fundamentally on hierarchies of race, class, gender, sexual orientation, and the like. Social justice activism risks becoming rigid and dogmatic, which makes it increasingly susceptible to becoming its own form of oppression and close-mindedness.

STOICISM AND REOPENING THE AMERICAN MIND

Thirty years before *The Coddling of the American Mind*, Allan Bloom wrote *The Closing of the American Mind*.[58] He began with a startling declaration: "There is one thing a professor can be absolutely certain of: almost every student entering the university believes, or says he believes, that truth is relative." Relativism, Bloom claimed, "is not a theoretical insight but a moral postulate, the condition of a free society, or so they see it."[59]

Students "have all been equipped with this framework early on, and it is the modern replacement for the inalienable natural rights that used to be the traditional American grounds for a free society." What students "fear from absolutism is not error but intolerance." Bloom identified a result that seems surprising for the Reagan era: "The point is not to correct [their] mistakes and really be right; rather it is not to think you are right at all."[60]

It is not necessarily surprising, however, when we consider that ideas have consequences long after they are introduced or become popularized. In the ensuing pages, Bloom argued that modern universities were failing their students in part because the enduring legacy of postmodern trends in the humanities had devalued the Western literary canon, which he championed as a tradition that honored and promoted the Socratic dictum that the unexamined life is not worth living.

In declaring that higher education had been so undermined that truth itself had been discarded as irrelevant or illegitimate by the best and the brightest at America's top universities, Bloom gave us a dire, perhaps unrealistic, account of the state of modern education. Whether or not things were as bad as he said, however, the book was a provocative contribution to an emerging conversation about social, political, and cultural values at a time when the ethos of multiculturalism was becoming a hot-button topic in institutions of higher learning and in society at large.

In Bloom's view, introspection was the point of a liberal education. He described the job of a teacher as a guide in this quest: "i.e., the delivery of real babies of which not the midwife but nature is the cause." A liberal education, he argued, helps students to develop a mature perspective and thoughtful position on universal questions about human nature—the most central being, what is man?—and "to become aware that the answer is neither obvious nor simply unavailable, and that there is no serious life in which this question is not a continuous concern."[61]

In invoking the Socratic dictum that the unexamined life is not worth living, the book also anchored its moral compass on the cultivation of character as one of the primary goals of a liberal education. Bloom was, not unlike the ancient Stoics, deriving inspiration from Socrates in advocating virtue, or excellence of character, as a fundamental goal of philosophical and intellectual inquiry. Indeed, one can envisage Bloom happily taking his cue from the Roman Stoic Seneca, who wrote that liberal studies do not give virtue, but "prepare the soul for the reception of virtue." They "do not conduct the soul all the way to virtue, but merely set it going in that direction" (*Letter* 88).

For Bloom, wrestling at a young age with timeless questions about human nature and the pursuit of the good life is an important moral foundation for civic life in general, and for the leadership of society in particular. Indeed, Bloom acknowledged that the sample of students upon which he had based his diagnosis of the present situation in American education was selective: "It consists of thousands of students of comparatively high intelligence, materially and spiritually free to do pretty much what they want with the few years of college they are privileged to have—in short, the kind of young persons who populate the twenty or thirty best universities."[62]

He made no apologies, however: "It is sometimes said that these advantaged youths have less need of our attention and resources, that they already have enough. But they, above all, most need education, in as much as the greatest talents are most difficult to perfect, and the more complex the nature the more susceptible it is to perversion."[63] Perhaps elitist in his attentiveness to "advantaged youths" and his insinuation that their complex nature requires the most attention lest their nature be perverted, Bloom was nonetheless encouraging pursuit of what the Stoics called *eudaimonia*. This notion refers to the state of happiness, or contentment with how one is living his life, that one reaches when one has excelled in the perfection, or completeness, of his character.

For Bloom, fulfillment in life seems to be sustainable only with the refinement of character and thought—one might say, virtue. For Bloom, a liberal education allows students to become familiar with the ideas of great thinkers in the past who have wrestled with the universal questions about human nature, society, and the ultimate question of how to live a good life. Among the great thinkers of the past were the ancient Hellenistic and Roman Stoics, for whom virtue was crucial.

On this last point, justice is one of the four cardinal virtues for not only the Stoics, but other ancient philosophies as well. As such, one might be inclined to think it should be a matter of utmost concern for "advantaged youths" at elite universities who are primed to become the leaders of tomorrow, especially since the pursuit of justice appears destined to be an ongoing work in progress, regardless of the time and place into which one is born. Hence, the need not only for guidance from wise elders, but for training in the cultivation of one's own moral compass.

In today's world of social justice activism, the convergence of mentoring and self-cultivation takes place on university campuses and other institutional settings in which much of the discussion is about a set of ideas that, as detailed above, underlie a particular way of talking about diversity and inclusion.

To wit: it is about identity politics.

This brand of politics—coming back to the "fragility" thesis of Haidt and Lukianoff—refers to a benign and productive effort to include a multiplicity of cultural perspectives in the canon of great literary and philosophical works. But it can also spark a more controversial politics of identity, tending to promote relativism and power politics, whereby truth, knowledge, and humanistic inquiry become inseparable from the relative "positionality" of identity, perspective, and institutional power.

A few years after Bloom's book appeared, historian Arthur Schlesinger Jr. published *The Disuniting of America: Reflections on a Multicultural Society*. A political liberal, Schlesinger warned of the dangers of identity politics. For example, he wrote: "The cult of ethnicity exaggerates differences, intensifies resentments and antagonisms, drives ever deeper the awful wedges between races and nationalities. The endgame is self-pity and self-ghettoization."[64]

Though he expressed optimism that unity would prevail in American society, his warning came as the Cold War ended, the Soviet Union broke apart, and ethnic separatism asserted itself in Eastern Europe. In America and abroad, it was an open question whether the ethos of multiculturalism in America, and ethnic separatism abroad, would lead to unity while broadening the circle of inclusion and pluralism, or greater division by kindling the tribal instincts of humanity.

As the discussion sometimes focused on the virtues of teaching "great books" by "dead White males," the relevance of a traditional liberal education was energizing enough to motivate film critic David Denby to write *Great Books*, in which he recounted a year he spent at Columbia University taking two core courses in the humanities focused on the great works of Western civilization. Denby wrote about coming away from the experience with a renewed appreciation for their insights into the human condition, and in so doing offered a defense of the Western literary canon.

Denby did not, however, neutralize a growing skepticism of the Western literary canon that had been taking root among intellectual elites who were among the precipitators of Bloom's dismay. Nor is it clear that Denby's celebration of the canon did anything to convince students at elite universities like Columbia University who, twenty-five years later, now presumably occupy positions of influence in institutions of politics, culture, and learning in American, and Western, society.

In a 1992 essay in the *New Criterion*, Roger Kimball reviewed a book by Julien Benda entitled *The Treason of the Intellectuals*, "an unremitting attack on the politicization of the intellect and ethnic separatism" published a decade before the outbreak of World War II. Applying Benda's observations to his own time, Mr. Kimball wrote: "From the savage flowering of ethnic hatreds in Eastern Europe and the former Soviet Union to the mendacious demands for political correctness and multiculturalism on college campuses across America and Europe, the treason of the intellectuals continues to play out its unedifying drama."[65]

Indeed, as Saul Bellow wrote in a foreword to Allan Bloom's book: "The heat of the dispute between Left and Right has grown so fierce in the last decade that the habits of civilized discourse have suffered a scorching."[66]

Mr. Bellow's words were written thirty years before Donald J. Trump was elected president of the United States.

Now we ask: how can Stoicism help?

NOTES

1. Jonathan Haidt and Greg Lukianoff, *The Coddling of the American Mind* (New York: Penguin, 2018), p. 6.

2. Jenny Jarvie, "Trigger Happy," *The New Republic,* March 3, 2014. Shannon Doyne, "Should Discomfort Excuse Students from Having to Complete an Assignment?," *New York Times*, The Learning Network blog, May 19, 2014.

3. David Denby, *Great Books* (New York: Simon & Schuster, 1996).

4. Jonathan Haidt and Greg Lukianoff, *The Coddling of the American Mind*, p. 6.

5. Jonathan Haidt and Greg Lukianoff, *The Coddling of the American Mind*, p. 7.

6. Jonathan Haidt and Greg Lukianoff, *The Coddling of the American Mind*, p. 9.

7. Jonathan Haidt and Greg Lukianoff, *The Coddling of the American Mind*, p. 9.

8. Jonathan Haidt and Greg Lukianoff, *The Coddling of the American Mind*, p. 10.

9. Jonathan Haidt and Greg Lukianoff, *The Coddling of the American Mind*, p. 9.

10. Donald Roberston, *The Philosophy of Cognitive-Behavioural Therapy: Stoic Philosophy as Rational and Cognitive Psychotherapy*, Second Edition (London, New York: Routledge, 2020).

11. Donald Robertson (with T. Codd), "Stoic Philosophy as a Cognitive-Behavioral Therapy," *Medium*, originally published in *The Behavior Therapist*, vol. 42, no. 2, February 2019. "Stoicism and the Art of Happiness: An Interview with Donald Robertson," *The Daily Stoic*, https://dailystoic.com/donald-robertson-interview/.

12. Massimo Pigliucci, *How to Be a Stoic: Using Ancient Philosophy to Live a Modern Life* (New York: Basic Books, 2017), pp. 9, 152.

13. Jonathan Haidt and Greg Lukianoff, *The Coddling of the American Mind*, pp. 94–96.

14. Jonathan Haidt and Greg Lukianoff, *The Coddling of the American Mind*, p. 95.

15. William Irvine, "How Would the Ancient Stoics Have Dealt with Hate Speech?," Oxford University Press blog, October 8, 2016, https://blog.oup.com/2016/10/stoic-philosophy-hate-speech/.

16. William Irvine, "How Would the Ancient Stoics Have Dealt with Hate Speech?," Oxford University Press blog, October 8, 2016, https://blog.oup.com/2016/10/stoic-philosophy-hate-speech/.

17. Margaret R. Graver, *Stoicism and Emotion*, p. 5.

18. Massimo Pigliucci and Gregory Lopez, *A Handbook for New Stoics: How to Thrive in a World Out of Your Control* (New York: The Experiment, 2019), audiobook (part 1, 4:32:00).

19. Donald Robertson, *How to Think Like a Roman Emperor*, p. 178.

20. Ibram X. Kendi, *Stamped from the Beginning* (New York: Bold Type Books, 2016), pp. 343–344.

21. Margaret Mitchell, *Gone with the Wind,* Pocket Book Edition, Macmillan edition published 1936 (New York: Simon & Schuster, 1936), p. 14.

22. Donald Robertson, *How to Think Like a Roman Emperor*, p. 181.

23. Derald Wing Sue, Christina M. Capodilupo, Gina C. Torino, Jennifer M. Bucceri, Aisha M. B. Holder, Kevin L. Nadal, and Marta Esquilin, "Racial Microaggressions in Everyday Life," *American Psychologist*, May–June 2007, vol. 62, no. 4, p. 271.

24. Black Students of Emory, "Black Students of Emory: A List of Demands," *The Emory Wheel*, December 2, 2015.

25. Peter Schmidt, "Occidental Faculty Weighs System for Reports of Microaggressions," *The Chronicle of Higher Education*, November 24, 2015.

26. "According to University of Wisconsin–Milwaukee Politically Correct is Offensive," November 7, 2015, https://mnrepublic.com/2613/uncategorized/according-to-university-of-wisconsin-milwaukee-politically-correct-is-offensive/.

27. Özlem Sensoy and Robin DiAngelo, *Is Everyone Really Equal?*, p. xviii.

28. Özlem Sensoy and Robin DiAngelo, *Is Everyone Really Equal?*, p. xviii.

29. Özlem Sensoy and Robin DiAngelo, *Is Everyone Really Equal?*, p. xix.

30. Özlem Sensoy and Robin DiAngelo, *Is Everyone Really Equal?*, p. 1.

31. Özlem Sensoy and Robin DiAngelo, *Is Everyone Really Equal?*, p. 4.

32. Rene Brouwer, *The Stoic Sage*, pp. 30–31. *Stoicism, Stanford Encyclopedia of Philosophy*, first published Monday April 15, 1996; substantive revision Tuesday April 10, 2018, https://plato.stanford.edu/entries/stoicism/. "[T]he Stoics do not maintain that the mere having of a cognitive impression constitutes knowledge (epistêmê). Indeed, not even assent to such an impression amounts to knowledge. Such assent is merely cognition or grasp (katalêpsis) of some individual fact. Real knowledge (epistêmê) requires cognition that is secure, firm and unchangeable by reason (Sextus Empiricus, 41C)—and, furthermore, worked into a systematic whole with other such cognitions (Arius Didymus, 41H)."

33. Özlem Sensoy and Robin DiAngelo, *Is Everyone Really Equal?*, p. 2.

34. Özlem Sensoy and Robin DiAngelo, *Is Everyone Really Equal?*, p. 5.

35. Douglas Kellner and Tyson Lewis, "Liberal Humanism and the European Critical Tradition," https://pages.gseis.ucla.edu/faculty/kellner/essays/libhumanism.pdf.

36. Matthew McManus, "What Is Critical Theory?," *Arc Digital,* April 30, 2021, https://polyarchy.arcdigital.media/p/what-is-critical-theory.

37. Douglas Kellner and Tyson Lewis, "Liberal Humanism and the European Critical Tradition," https://pages.gseis.ucla.edu/faculty/kellner/essays/libhumanism.pdf, pp. 32–37.

38. Helen Pluckrose and James Lindsay, *Cynical Theories: How Activist Scholarship Made Everything about Race, Gender, and Identity—and Why This Harms Everybody* (Durham, NC: Pitchstone, 2020).

39. Herbert Marcuse, "Repressive Tolerance," from Robert Paul Wolff, Barrington Moore Jr., and Herbert Marcuse, *A Critique of Pure Tolerance* (Boston: Beacon

Press, 1969), pp. 95–137. https://www.marcuse.org/herbert/publications/1960s/1965-repressive-tolerance-fulltext.html.

40. Jonathan Haidt and Greg Lukianoff, *The Coddling of the American Mind*, pp. 62–67.

41. Bryan Burroughs, *Days of Rage: America's Radical Underground, the FBI, and the Forgotten Age of Revolutionary Violence* (New York: Penguin, 2015). Isaac Gottesman, *The Critical Turn in Education: From Marxist Critique to Poststructuralist Feminism to Critical Theories of Race* (New York, London: Routledge, 2016).

42. Paulo Freire, *Pedagogy of the Oppressed* (New York: Bloomsbury, 1970). Antonio Gramsci, *Prison Notebooks* (London: Electric Book Company, 1999).

43. Richard Delgado and Jean Stefancic, *Critical Race Theory: The Cutting Edge*, p. 2.

44. Richard Delgado and Jean Stefancic, *Critical Race Theory: The Cutting Edge*, p. 2.

45. Richard Delgado and Jean Stefancic, *Critical Race Theory: An Introduction* (New York: New York University Press, 2017), p. 5.

46. Michael Minnicino, "The New Dark Age: The Frankfurt School and 'Political Correctness,'" The Schiller Institute, *Fidelio Magazine*, Winter 1992.

47. Martin Jay, "Dialectic of Counter-Enlightenment: The Frankfurt School as Scapegoat of the Lunatic Fringe," *Canadian Institute for the Study of Antisemitism*, December 22, 2011.

48. George F. Will, "The End of Our Holiday from History," *Washington Post*, September 12, 2001.

49. Jonathan Haidt and Greg Lukianoff, *The Coddling of the American Mind*, pp. 110–111, citing research conducted by the Higher Education Research Institute.

50. Max Horkheimer, *Critical Theory: Selected Essays*, p. 197.

51. Max Horkheimer, *Critical Theory: Selected Essays*, p. 196.

52. Max Horkheimer, *Critical Theory: Selected Essays*, p. 200.

53. Max Horkheimer, *Critical Theory: Selected Essays*, p. 200.

54. Manning Marable, "Beyond Racial Identity Politics: Towards a Liberation Theory for Multicultural Democracy," chapter in *Privileging Positions: The Sites of Asian American Studies*, edited by Gary Y. Okihiro et al. (Washington State University Board of Regents, 1995). Reprinted in Richard Delgado and Jean Stefancic, *Critical Race Theory: The Cutting Edge*, p. 590.

55. Kimberlée Crenshaw, "Demarginalizing the Intersection of Race and Sex: A Black Feminist Critique of Antidiscrimination Doctrine, Feminist Theory and Antiracist Politics," University of Chicago Legal Forum, Volume 1989, Issue 1, Article 8, p. 140.

56. Kimberlé Crenshaw, "Why Intersectionality Can't Wait," *The Washington Post*, September 24, 2015. Kimberlée Crenshaw, "Demarginalizing the Intersection of Race and Sex: A Black Feminist Critique of Antidiscrimination Doctrine, Feminist Theory and Antiracist Politics," University of Chicago Legal Forum, Volume 1989, Issue 1, Article 8.

57. Manning Marable, "Beyond Racial Identity Politics: Towards a Liberation Theory for Multicultural Democracy," chapter in *Privileging Positions: The Sites of*

Asian American Studies, edited by Gary Y. Okihiro et al. (Washington State University Board of Regents, 1995). Reprinted in Richard Delgado and Jean Stefancic, *Critical Race Theory: The Cutting Edge*, p. 590.

58. Allan Bloom, *The Closing of the American Mind* (New York: Simon & Schuster, 1987).

59. Allan Bloom, *The Closing of the American Mind*, p. 25.

60. Allan Bloom, *The Closing of the American Mind*, pp. 25–26.

61. Allan Bloom, *The Closing of the American Mind*, pp. 20–21.

62. Allan Bloom, *The Closing of the American Mind*, p. 22.

63. Allan Bloom, *The Closing of the American Mind*, p. 22.

64. Arthur M. Schlesinger Jr., *The Disuniting of America: Reflections on a Multicultural Society*, Revised and Enlarged Edition (London, New York: W. W. Norton & Company, 1998, 1992, 1991), p. 106.

65. Roger Kimball, "The Treason of the Intellectuals & 'The Undoing of Thought,'" *The New Criterion*, December 1992.

66. Allan Bloom, *The Closing of the American Mind*, p. 18.

Chapter 3

The Philosophy of Stoicism

Stoicism was one of several influential philosophies that emerged in the ancient world. Originating in the city-state of Athens during the age of Alexander the Great, and lasting until the death of the Roman emperor Marcus Aurelius, Stoic philosophy spanned five centuries and often had considerable clout at the highest levels of the Roman Empire (at least when Stoic philosophers were not being exiled by a Roman emperor). But a question arises: how can a philosophy that thrived in the Hellenistic period of many centuries ago have any relevance in the world today? What does it have to offer in the quest for social justice in the twenty-first century?

The answer begins with one word: virtue. As we will see below, in the words of ancient biographer Diogenes Laertius, the Stoics believed that virtue "is a harmonious disposition, and should be chosen for its own sake, not out of fear or hope or with reference to anything external." Virtue is "a certain perfection" that is the foundation of happiness in life, "since virtue is the state of mind that makes the whole of life harmonious."[1] This harmonious disposition of virtue provides a basis for the distinction we encountered in the introduction between the living of one's life and the circumstances of one's life. Living virtuously is the key to autonomy and contentment. In virtuous autonomy, we also find the basis for moral agency on behalf of social justice.

In chapter 1, we saw how autonomy was the central concern of the Frankfurt School. The development of Critical Theory was in large part a response to the Frankfurt School's belief that, in the modern world of capitalism, humanity was in a state of alienation. Their critique of capitalist institutions and ideology explained how the bifurcation of reason into instrumental and objective reason (the "eclipse of reason") had stripped human beings of their autonomy and left them in a state of false consciousness.

The aim of Critical Theory was to diagnose the social and ideological circumstances that underpin alienation. Rational autonomy was the end goal, but to reach that goal, it was necessary to overcome the eclipse of reason and begin making proper use of objective reason to diagnose and remove the

conditions of alienation (oppression). Only in clearing the social and ideological circumstances underpinning alienation (oppression) could human beings
flourish and reach their full potential. In ensuing decades, this basic idea then
extended into numerous fields of study including postcolonial studies, queer
theory, critical race theory, and feminism.

The ancient Stoics were committed to virtue as the key to happiness. For
the Stoics, however, the cultivation of virtue in one's character is prior to the
transformation of our institutions if we are to achieve autonomy and go about
making the world a better place. The effective use of reason in pursuit of
virtue is essential in the quest for autonomy and social justice.

At its core, Stoicism is a *eudaimonistic* philosophy that claims that virtue
is sufficient for a life of lasting happiness (autonomy). *Eudaimonia* can be
translated as "happiness," "flourishing," "fulfillment," "well-being," or the
"good life."[2] As a *eudaimonistic* philosophy, Stoicism is designed to help
us live better lives, both as individuals in our own right and as members of
the human community. Though the Greek founders of Stoicism were deeply
involved in working out its core theoretical principles, Stoicism evolved into
an eminently practical philosophy, especially as it became widely adopted
during the Roman Empire. It was a philosophy of life, focused on the cultivation of virtue as the foundation of good character and ethical maturation.

In focusing on character, the Stoic conception of virtue emphasizes the
moral worth and dignity of each human being. It also stresses the responsibility of each human being for cultivating his or her virtue as the condition for
his or her own happiness, and for contributing to the betterment of his or her
society. This worldview encourages us to be better people, in terms of treating
others with dignity and respect as a first step in contributing to the improvement of society. Stoicism also provides us with a set of intellectual tools that
help minimize the anxieties that we might suffer by worrying about the social
circumstances in which we find ourselves.

This worldview arises from a naturalistic conception of the universe, of
which human beings are an integral part. In the attempt to understand the
workings and ethical implications of this universe, there are three areas of
inquiry to pursue: physics, logic, and ethics. According to one guide to stoicism, logic deals with the form and expression of knowledge; physics deals
with the matter of knowledge; and ethics deals with the use of knowledge.[3]
The idea is that an understanding of how nature works, combined with the
application of sound human reasoning, leads to the development of an ethical
character centered on the cultivation of four cardinal virtues: wisdom, courage, temperance, and courage. These virtues are derived from Socrates, a
foundational influence on the philosophy of Stoicism.

Some scholars suggest the analogy of an egg to help understand how these
themes work together. The yolk of an egg represents physics. The white of

the egg represents ethics. The shell is the logic. Physics refers to how nature works, and it lies at the core of Stoicism because you cannot have a guide for ethical behavior without knowing how events in the universe are determined. Once you have a framework in place to guide ethical behavior, logic provides the hard reasoning that solidifies the will in its decision to undertake a course of action determined to be virtuous. Stoic author Massimo Pigliucci suggests another analogy that is perhaps even clearer:

> The best simile in my mind is that of a garden: the fence is the Logic—defending the precious inside and defining its boundaries; the fertile soil is the Physics—providing the nutritive power by way of knowledge of the world; and the resulting fruits are the Ethics—the actual focal objective of Stoic teachings.[4]

These three themes together constitute an integrated framework for studying how we can bring ourselves, through the cultivation of virtue, into harmony with the Logos underlying the universe.

First, we learn about the universe, which, as Stoic expert Anthony Long explains, is "a determinate structure, a closed system of causes and effects, where nothing is simply random or by chance." This implies that "every external situation we face could not be otherwise than what it is," bound to be for us and our circumstances. At the same time, fate is not assigned to us independently of who we are and what we do. "We co-determine our fate by the decisions we undertake and by the responses we give to our circumstances." This co-determination implies serious responsibility on our part to act on those aspects of our lives that are under our control.[5]

Second, as we conduct our study of physics, logic, and ethics, we learn how to apply the four cardinal virtues in those aspects of our lives that are under our control. This endeavor necessarily involves the deployment of human reason in coordination with ongoing work on what French scholar Pierre Hadot calls the disciplines of desire, action, and assent. The discipline of desire calls on us to desire only what nature affords us—coming to terms with our fate. The discipline of action calls on us to love our fellow human beings as members of a common humanity and thus doing our best to help everyone flourish as "fate" may permit. The discipline of assent calls on us to rely on the rational faculty conferred to us by nature to assent only to objectively true value judgments about the impressions of reality that present themselves to our mind.

On the discipline of assent, Stoic author and cognitive-behavioral therapist Donald Robertson writes:

> By continually monitoring their judgements, Stoics are to notice the early-warning signs of upsetting or unhealthy impressions and take a step back from them,

withholding their "assent" or agreement, rather than being "carried away" into irrational and unhealthy passions and the vices.[6]

As creatures endowed by nature with reason, human beings are an integral part of a naturalistic universe that itself is immanently rational. For the Stoics, there is no difference between God and nature. The Stoics conceive of God (i.e., nature) as Logos. The idea is that reason is the underlying organizing principle guiding the workings of the universe. Understanding the physics of this universe through the application of logic is key to Stoic ethics. This ethic ultimately involves living in accord with nature, which is akin living in accord with reason.

This naturalistic view, rooted in a biological rather than mechanistic conception of the universe, leads to a deterministic view of human affairs that is nevertheless compatible with free will because human reason, and thus human agency, is itself a causal force working in tandem with the universe.

The role of reason in Stoic philosophy is grounded in a representational theory of knowledge and a correspondence theory of truth. The impressions of reality (*phantasia*) that present themselves to consciousness are subject to rational evaluation. Reason judges whether they are true or false impressions of reality. If true, we have cognition, which becomes "real knowledge (epistêmê)" when cognition "is secure, firm and unchangeable by reason." This doesn't mean that reason cannot commit errors in reasoning. Rather, as Dirk Baltzly explains, it means that "it is within our power to avoid falling into error and that there is a kind of impression which reveals to us the world as it really is and which is different from those impressions which might not so reveal the world."[7]

This introductory summary of Stoicism highlights the essential task performed by reason in managing the interplay between the living of our lives and the circumstances of our lives. As noted in the introduction, this distinction between the living of our lives and the circumstances of our lives is crucial to understanding how Stoicism offers a viable alternative to Critical Social Justice.

Stoicism shares with Critical Social Justice a fundamental concern with improving the circumstances of life for all human beings, though it differs from Critical Social Justice in shifting the focus from identity groups to the idea that there is a common humanity to which we all belong. But as suggested in the introduction, Stoicism emphasizes intent rather than impact, *without* neglecting impact, as the anchor on which to center moral agency in the quest for social justice. That is, it is in living our lives as virtuously as we can that we can reliably improve the circumstances of life in the long-term, both for ourselves and for others who share the world with us.

Virtuous living is also autonomous living. It focuses on the thing we can control—trying to live virtuously—and not on what the Stoics called "externals," or things that are outside our control and thus are not a matter of virtue. It is vital to point out, however, that the Stoics were not like the ancient Cynics, for whom virtue was the *only* consideration in life. The Stoics did not disavow or discourage the acquisition of wealth, cultivation of good health, and other "pleasures" in life. They also did not fault us for trying to avoid poverty, illness, and other "pains" in life.

They did, however, refer to these pleasures and pains as aspects of life about which we should be "indifferent" in relation to the central importance of virtue. They distinguished between "preferred indifferents" and "dispreferred indifferents." Health and wealth are generally preferred, while poverty and illness are generally not preferred. But health and wealth can be misused, while poverty and illness can provide opportunities to manifest virtue. In the latter case, for example, living life as productively as possible while dealing with illness requires endurance, a form of courage.

The key insight is that reason guides us to an assessment of how to make use of pleasures and pains virtuously. Health and wealth are circumstances in our lives. Whether we use them virtuously involves the living of our lives. It is the latter that falls within the realm of our autonomy.

The notion that rationality guides us to virtue arises from what Professor Anthony Long, who has had a long career in the study of Stoic philosophy, describes as the three "reciprocal, doctrinal principles" that run consistently through the Greek and Roman periods of the ancient school of Stoic philosophy:[8]

1. The rational and providential structure of the universe;
2. The special status, responsibilities, and challenges of being a human being endowed with reason; and
3. The innate potentiality and goal of human beings to live well together in all circumstances.

These principles begin with Zeno of Citium. As noted in chapter 1, Zeno is credited as the founder of Stoicism after losing a fortune of purple dye in a shipwreck. A one-time merchant who sold the purple dye used to adorn the imperial robes, Zeno once got caught in a storm while transporting his valuable commodity from Phoenicia to Piraeus. Having once been told by the Delphic oracle, whose cryptic advice on fate was held in high esteem by the ancient Greeks, to "take on the color not of dead shellfish but of dead men,"[9] he subsequently found himself in a bookseller's shop and heard the bookseller reading a book about Socrates. He was so struck by what he was reading that he asked the bookseller where he could find a person like Socrates.

As fate would have it, the Cynic philosopher Crates was strolling past the bookstore. The bookseller advised Zeno to seek Crates.

Zeno soon came under the tutelage of Crates, and eventually founded his own school of Stoicism, named for the *stoa poikile*, or "painted porch," in which he preached to his students. Zeno first laid out a basic principle of Stoic teaching that the essence of virtue is to "live consistently."

His successor as head of the Stoic school, Cleanthes, subsequently clarified that to live consistently is to live in agreement with nature.[10] Stoicism is driven in large part by an interest in what a person ought to do in life (it is a philosophy of life describing how one ought to live), and what one ought to do in life is a function of how we relate to nature. In this view, living in accord with nature blurs, if not dissolves, the modern distinction between "is" and "ought." What we ought to do reflects who we are as creatures endowed by nature with reason. As such, virtue is paramount.

VIRTUE IN A RATIONAL AND NATURALISTIC UNIVERSE

The Stoics developed various ideas about virtue, some theoretical and some practical, some intellectual and some nonintellectual, some primary and some secondary. The primary virtues are wisdom, justice, self-control, and courage—derived from Socrates, who was a foundational influence on the Stoics. The primary vices, which are to be avoided, are foolishness, injustice, intemperance, and cowardice. According to Diogenes Laertius, for the Stoics, virtue "is a harmonious disposition, and should be chosen for its own sake, not out of fear or hope or with reference to anything external." Virtue is "a certain perfection" that is the foundation of happiness in life, "since virtue is the state of mind that makes the whole of life harmonious."[11]

As such, says Diogenes, virtue "and that which participates in it are said to be good" in being the source, manner, and agent of the benefit conferred. The man who "participates in virtue" is good, which is defined as "the natural perfection of a rational being as such." Although virtue is to be pursued for its own sake, it is the case that the byproduct of virtuous actions are "joy, cheerfulness, and the like."[12]

For the Stoic Ariston of Chios, "the goal was to live in a state of indifference to everything that is intermediate between virtue and vice." Similarly, for Herillus of Chalcedon, anything between virtue and vice was to be regarded as an indifferent.[13]

As explained in a wonderfully comprehensive lecture by the late philosophy professor Arthur Holmes,[14] Stoicism provides an ethical framework according to which virtue is pursued for its own sake rather than for the "external" benefits it confers (which would be a "consequentialist" ethical system). It is based on the laws and obligations that nature imposes on us as rational beings, and to live in accordance with the course of nature is to be in harmony with the Logos, or structured order of the universe. The presumption is that taking nature as your starting point is itself natural, not perverse. Only "externals" can pervert your motives and actions.

For the Stoics, says Holmes, pleasure is not to be pursued for its own sake. It is, at best, a "fringe benefit" accompanying virtue (he might have added, as discussed above, that pleasure is typically seen as a "preferred indifferent" to be used virtuously). All of this flows from the Stoic view of the cosmos as a rational order in which nothing outside of our own will is "good" or "bad," and things within reach of our will are "good" or "bad" insofar as we employ the faculty of reason bestowed by nature to exercise judgment. Our will, or *prohairesis*, is the power by which we cultivate the four principal virtues and seek to live in harmony with nature: courage, moderation, justice, and wisdom.

We now have a philosophical basis for the Roman Stoic Epictetus's insistence that people are disturbed not by things but by the opinions they form of things. Reason not only guides us to virtue but provides us with the power of judgment. We can thus reconcile a seeming conflict between the urge to regard Stoicism as a philosophy of free will and as a philosophy of determinism.

As a philosophy that urges us to live in harmony with what one may regard as the iron laws of nature that are beyond our control, Stoicism is a deterministic philosophy. But the ability of reason to form judgments that guide our will (*prohairesis*) also implies the freedom implicit in the Stoic advice to use reason to train oneself to form correct judgments about nature and one's place in it. In other words, our rational decision-making is one of the "laws" by which the universe carries out its "will."

A Stoic concept that helps clarify this compatibility is *oikeiosis*. As explained by Massimo Pigliucci on the Internet Encyclopedia of Philosophy , *oikeiosis* is "often translated as affinity, or appropriation." This means that "human beings have natural propensities to develop morally, propensities that begin as what we today would call instincts and can then be greatly refined with the onset of the age of reason at the childhood stage and beyond." Reason is a part of who we are and is meant to be (should be) used to bring ourselves into alignment with nature. If so, we can thrive as individuals in our own right and as human beings contributing to the betterment of a common humanity. As Pigliucci notes, "this naturalistic account of the roots of virtuous/moral behavior is highly compatible with modern findings in both evolutionary and cognitive science."[15]

Continuing with the basic tenets of Stoicism as summarized in a lecture by the late Arthur Holmes, Stoicism is rooted in Cynicism in its emotional "detachment from external circumstances"—"comforts and troubles" that lie beyond our control. To get in harmony with nature, the Stoics embrace *apatheia*, or indifference to anything not connected with the cultivation of virtue on the path to *eudaimonia*. The cultivation of virtue depends on one's will and reason, which also facilitate the development of *ataraxia*, the serenity achieved from caring only about the things you can control (although we should note that *ataraxia* is more associated with the Epicureans, *apatheia* with the Stoics).[16]

It is important to emphasize, however, that neither *apatheia* nor *ataraxia* implies that the Stoics sought to close themselves off from the world. Far from it. Stoicism, notes Professor Long, "was designed for action in the world," and "according to the Stoic doctrine, the wise man will engage in public life if the opportunity arises." Cato the Younger, for example, was an exemplary manifestation of the worldly Stoic philosopher (Cato's Stoic disposition was well-known in his lifetime and became even more well-known when he committed suicide to avoid surrendering to Julius Caesar).[17] We will see a similar example with the Stoic-like Abraham Lincoln in the final chapter.

More generally, says Holmes, Stoics were realists who did not shy away from the reality that adversity, trouble, and challenge are inevitable parts of our lives. They are a natural law in themselves. The idea of *apatheia* is not to shut yourself off from these challenges, but to order your life in such a way that you are able to harmonize with them in healthy and productive ways. This means ordering your life in accord with the laws and obligations nature imposes on us as rational beings.

This worldview stems from a pantheistic view of the cosmos in which nature is a unified whole, with things running contrary to nature being "evil" and things being in harmony with nature being "good." Nature has active and passive aspects, the former being rational (soul) and the latter being material (body), or, as Diogenes Laertius says, matter ("unqualified substance").[18] The rational, or providential, part is associated with God, or Logos, an active force known as cosmic reason (Anaxagoras called it "nous," while Heraclitus called it "logos").

This makes nature an ordered, intelligible process in which, according to Homes, "natural laws are causal forces at work in nature." Nature is not immaterial or transcendent, but a material, biological being in which all that exists are particulars of various sizes and composite natures. Indeed, in *Origins of Stoic Cosmology*, David Hahm writes: "No idea is more deeply ingrained in Stoic philosophy than the conviction that everything real is corporeal. This notion is found in Stoic logic, epistemology, cosmology, psychology, theology, and ethics, in fact, wherever the Stoics discussed what they believed to be real."[19]

To round out the details, the four basic elements are fire, air, earth, and water. As described by Margaret Graver, "the elements air and fire are like each other in that both are considered 'active' elements which work together upon the two 'passive' elements, water and earth." The combination of fire and air "produces 'tension' (tonos) by the balance of opposed forces, and this tension may vary in intensity, like the varying vibrations in the strings of a musical instrument."[20]

"It is variations in tension, and not the properties of air and fire alone, that explain differences in the qualities imparted by *pneuma* to things," such as hardness to stones or whiteness to silver.[21] *Pneuma* is "the animating mind-stuff,"[22] or "designing fire,"[23] which constitutes "one of the two un-generated and indestructible first principles (*archai*) of the universe."[24] These two principles are the "utterly unqualified and inert" matter which is acted upon, and the "intelligent designing fire or a breath (*pneuma*) which structures matter in accordance" with the plan of God, or eternal reason (Logos).[25]

The upshot is that the starting points of nature are never perverse. Nature is given to us, and it is our job to work within the constraints of nature. To the extent we have the capacity to work within these constraints to beneficial effects, we are creatures of nature. As such, we are responsible for reflecting on our own individual personalities and capabilities to determine how we might work within these natural constraints. The constraints are external factors, or circumstances that do not stem from one's own will, which can pervert our motives and actions if we fail to exert the agency that reason avails to us to determine how these circumstances will affect us.

In this natural order, or "Logos nature," according to Holmes, the most basic starting point (instinct) for humanity and animals is self-preservation. It is not pleasure, which is only a by-product that emerges when "nature has found the means suitable for continued existence."[26] After that, "nature's rule (for animals) is to follow the direction of impulse."[27] On humanity, however, nature has bestowed reason, which "supervenes to shape impulse" by means of the acquisition of knowledge.[28]

Reason, then, is fundamental for human beings. It distinguishes human beings from other living beings. The benefit reason confers to humankind gives rise to a representational theory of knowledge whereby ideas are representations of impressions implanted on consciousness by external objects. This differs from the Platonic conception of innate knowledge and the Aristotelian conception of potential intellect.

This consciousness, or tabula rasa (blank slate), instead foreshadows the British and European empiricisms of the seventeenth and eighteenth centuries, in which you are aware of ideas of impressions rather than the objects that produce the impressions. The criterion by which you determine whether your ideas are accurate representations of external objects is, like with René Descartes and Baruch Spinoza in the seventeenth century, whether the ideas are clear and distinct.

In short, humans are endowed by nature with reason.

It is reason that gives us our special capacity to figure out how to live in harmony with nature. This brings us back to the beginning of Stoicism. For Zeno and his immediate follower Cleanthes, a life lived in agreement with the dictates of nature is a life of virtue. Chrysippus, who followed Cleanthes, talks about universal nature and the nature of man, disregarding individual natures as susceptible to the distortions of passion. Because virtue is a disposition whereby one harmoniously abides the course of nature, the embrace of virtue is a "choice worthy for its own sake, intrinsically good, not from hope or fear of any external motive."[29] It is an ethic of "what I ought to do, what natural law requires, what my duty is, rather than an ethic of desired consequences,"[30] making pleasure only "a fringe benefit, not something to be pursued for its own sake."[31]

THE THREE DISCIPLINES

The wise man, embracing virtue, is passionless because he grasps the nature of his circumstances without hope, fear, or anxiety. Of course, perfect wisdom is likely unreachable for most, if not all, of us, but it is quite within our capacity to strive for wisdom. In this quest, Epictetus and Marcus Aurelius provide us with a systematic guide by introducing and explicating the "disciplines" of desire, action, and assent—what Pierre Hadot identifies as three fundamental "exercise themes" of Stoicism.[32] These "three activities or operations of the soul" involve cultivating habits of desire, action, and judgment that stem from "the delimitation of our own sphere of liberty as an impregnable islet of autonomy, in the midst of the vast river of events and of Destiny."

> What depends on us are thus the acts of our soul, because we can freely choose them. We can judge or not judge, or judge in whatever manner we please; we can desire or not desire; will or not will.[33][34]

As Donald Robertson notes, Hadot describes the *discipline of desire* in terms of *amor fati*, or loving one's fate.[35] "Demand not that events should happen as you wish," Epictetus said, "but wish them to happen as they do happen, and you will go on well" (*Enchiridion*, VIII). To repeat a previous point, *amor fati* does not mean the wise man is passive and resigned. Rather, he seeks to desire only that which is in accord with his place in the structured world of the cosmos. It is a matter of wisdom to discover and recognize what that place is. When Darnella Frazier recorded the video of George Floyd's killing, she was not trying to reconcile with Mr. Floyd's killing but discovering her role in the cause of justice.

The discipline of desire is accompanied by the *discipline of action*, which means, in the words of Hadot (speaking for Epictetus and Marcus Aurelius), "the goal of our actions must be the good of the human community, and the discipline of action will therefore have as its domain our relations with other people." Coming back to the interplay between intent and impact, "what gives an action its completeness," writes Hadot, "is precisely the moral intention by which it is inspired, not the subject matter on which it is exercised."[36]

> With the appearance of reason in human beings, natural instinct becomes reflective choice. At this stage, we recognize *rationally* which things have "value," since they correspond to the innate tendencies that nature has placed within us.[37]

At last, we arrive at the *discipline of assent*, or judgment, which "consists essentially in refusing to accept within oneself all representations which are other than objective or adequate."[38] To strive for virtue as rational beings is to work consistently on the disciplines of desire, action, and assent, which have to do, as Donald Robertson summarizes, with the acceptance of our fate, love of mankind, and mindfulness of our judgments.[39] In short, the Stoics did not just describe virtue. They mapped out a whole plan for going about the cultivation of virtue.

The disciplines of desire, action, and assent arise from the physics, ethics, and logic that underlie the Stoic philosophical worldview. With the cultivation of the four cardinal, interconnected virtues of wisdom, courage, temperance, and justice, we move closer to a state of harmony with a rational cosmos in which proper reasoning (logic) facilitates our arrival at an understanding of how nature works (physics) and provides us with a basis for moral agency (ethics).

To repeat, reason guides us to virtue, which is the key to *eudaimonia* (the well-lived life) and *ataraxia* (peace of mind). Integrating the four cardinal virtues into our lives is how we can best contribute to a more harmonious disposition of human affairs. The virtues are also integral to the quest for social justice. In the exercise of wisdom, courage, temperance, and justice, we focus on the living of our lives—cultivating good character, as well as resilience in the face of life's challenges and obstacles. We also focus on discovering the unique ways each of us can contribute to social justice.

When Darnella Frazier had the presence of mind (wisdom) to film Derek Chauvin with his knee on the neck of George Floyd, had the self-control (temperance) to keep the film running, and the courage to hand over her phone to the authorities in the interest of justice, she was exhibiting Stoic virtue in action. She exemplified virtuous (autonomous) action in the quest for social justice.

DICHOTOMY OF CONTROL

One of the most famous stories in the history of Stoicism is about a broken leg. The Roman Stoic philosopher, Epictetus, was born a slave (his name means "acquired" in Greek) in modern-day Turkey, when it was under the control of the Roman Empire. In his childhood, he was sold to Epaphroditus, a man who had once been a slave himself but who became a wealthy freedman and went on to join the Stoic philosopher Seneca as a member of Emperor Nero's imperial administration, in the role of secretary. Accounts vary about the overall treatment of Epictetus under Epaphroditus, but one thing seems to be clear: Epaphroditus broke Epictetus's leg.

He may not have meant to break the leg, but he did take hold of Epictetus's leg and twist it so hard that Epictetus warned him that the leg would break if Epaphroditus persisted. Epictetus issued the warning with remarkable poise and calm, stating in a matter-of-fact way that if Epaphroditus kept applying the pressure, the bone in his leg would snap. Sure enough, it did. Epictetus's reaction was merely to remind Epaphroditus that he had issued the warning. In other words: I told you so.

It seems a strange reaction, almost as if the victim, in saying *I told you so*, were claiming victory. But in a sense, Epictetus was claiming victory. The reason for this tells us a lot about the dichotomy of control, one of the most significant applied principles to come out of Stoicism and one that Epictetus would go on to consistently preach when he became a freedman and philosopher.

The first thing to note is that Epictetus lived the rest of his life with a limp, which presumably was due to the lingering effects of the broken leg. Donald Robertson writes that Epictetus regarded his lameness as "an impediment to the leg but not to the mind." That is, "Epictetus was no more perturbed by his crippled leg than he was by his inability to grow wings and fly—he simply accepted it as one of the many things in life that were beyond his control."[40] Epictetus was one of the three most influential Roman Stoics (the others being Seneca and Marcus Aurelius), and he forthrightly articulated many of the basic principles of Stoic philosophy.

As he is recorded saying by Flavius Arrian in the *Enchridion* (Manual): "There are things which are within our power, and there are things which are beyond our power" (*Enchiridion*, I). Epictetus had control over the actions he could undertake that, to the best of his ability, he believed would not so upset

Epaphroditus that the latter would be moved to twist his leg until it broke. But he had no control over how Epaphroditus would react. Epaphroditus might have been in a bad mood or there may have been other "external factors" (factors unrelated to Epictetus's own will) that motivated Epaphroditus to break the leg. For Epictetus, you should only be concerned with what you can control.

On what possible worldview could Epictetus acclimate himself to a "dichotomy of control" mindset by which he could avoid getting upset about having his leg broken by his master Epaphroditus? As noted, the Stoics held a naturalistic view of the world, based on the idea of a rational order, or Logos, in the universe. To put it briefly, the Logos refers to the Stoic conception of God as an intelligence, or rationality, that does not transcend the universe, but is immanent within the universe—God is not separate from the universe but is the universe itself. Moreover, God is a living intelligence that is morally good, omnipotent, rational, and sentient.

Everything that happens in the universe is interconnected with other happenings in the universe as a result of deterministic relationships that include the causal connections between our choices and the consequences of our choices. In other words, notions of free will and determinism, familiar to us in the contemporary world, are compatible because rational human beings are an integral part of the rational Logos.

Our rationality is a manifestation of the rationality of the universe. As rational beings, we have an obligation to understand this world and to live in harmony with it. To do so is to move us closer to living a life of virtue, understood as excellence of character. This does not mean that accepting his pain made Epictetus immune to pain. It means instead that, once the leg was broken, nothing was to be gained from stewing in anger about it.

Stoicism is not about training oneself not to feel the pain that one naturally feels as a physiological creature. We can safely assume that Epictetus felt searing pain when the bone in his leg snapped. It is about emotional resilience. Epictetus walked with a lifelong limp, but presumably unlike most of us would, he did not complain about his broken leg. He accepted that it was there and did the best he could. It is a misconception about Stoicism to see it as a philosophy of resignation. Indeed, as Stoic advisor Arius wrote to Roman Emperor Augustus Caesar's wife Livia after the loss of her son Drusus, "there is nothing that fastens such a reproach on Fortune as resignation."[41]

Professor Anthony Long has explicitly insisted that "action, not resignation, least of all self-absorption, was the original driver of the Stoic movement."[42] Stoicism is not a philosophy that demands we passively resign ourselves to every arbitrary decree of nature. It demands instead that we live up to the potential that nature affords to us, which is not the same as resigning ourselves to nature.

Further, Professor Long continues, the "past, up to the last second, is settled, and therefore no grounds for rational regret or congratulation, but our future will depend crucially on how we decide to act."[43] Epictetus would have preferred that Epaphroditus not break his leg, but once it was broken, and likely being without access to doctors, Epictetus could only let his body mend the leg as best as possible while continuing to live as virtuously as possible. Epictetus's broken leg exemplifies the dichotomy of control not as a central tenet in a philosophy of complacency, but in a philosophy of action anchored on the virtues to which reason guides us. Reason underlies what Pierre Hadot calls "the extraordinary unity which held the parts of the Stoic system together."[44]

As described by Émile Bréhier, quoted by Pierre Hadot:

> It is one single, unique reason which, in dialectics, links consequent propositions to their antecedents; which, in nature, links together all causes; and which, in human conduct, establishes perfect concord between acts. It is impossible that a good man should not be a physicist and a dialectician; it is impossible for rationality to be realized separately in these three areas; it is impossible completely to grasp the reason within the course of events in the universe without, at the same time, realizing reason within one's own behavior.[45]

Epictetus's broken leg, and the way he handled it, helps illustrate the Stoic principle of the dichotomy of control as it pertains to the Stoic conception of a rational Logos underlying a naturalistic universe in which our choices and our circumstances are co-determined. Living in accord with nature is about knowing how to make the best of a situation (wisdom), when it is necessary to endure (courage), not to wallow in self-pity (temperance), and finally, how to help others (justice).

Coming back to social justice, *Being Better* authors Kai Whiting and Leonidas Konstantakos write cogently that "while it is true that complaining and wallowing in self-pity is fundamentally un-Stoic, taking action to solve a problem, say by joining a protest in the face of vice, is one of many possible Stoic responses."[46] Living in accord with nature, as beings endowed by nature with the faculty of reason, means using what nature has given us (reason) to make the right decisions in response to the challenges, obstacles, and adversities that circumstances present to us. They quote a trenchant insight by contemporary philosopher Alain de Botton:[47]

> We can as easily go astray by accepting the unnecessary and denying the possible, as by denying the necessary and wishing, for the impossible. It is for reason to make the decision.

Epictetus could deny the necessity of learning how to get on with life after his leg was broken and wish for the impossibility of turning back to clock to prevent getting his leg broken. He could also unnecessarily accept a judgment that he deserved to have his leg broken or deny the possibility of continuing to act virtuously in conducting his own affairs in life. It is for reason to work it all out. In so doing, reason allows us to aim for the highest perfection of which we are capable: virtue.

STOICISM AND CRITICAL SOCIAL JUSTICE

Epictetus not only talked the talk, but literally walked the walk. In talking the talk, Epictetus stressed one of the most fundamental life lessons that comes out of the role of virtue in Stoic philosophy, known as the "dichotomy of control." As he famously taught, we have no control over "externals" such as health, wealth, and other factors that are not a fundamental feature of character. But we do have control over the choices we make and the opinions we form about the things that happen to us. As a slave, Epictetus might not have had control over Epaphroditus when the latter was twisting his leg, but he did have control over how he thought about it.

How should he have thought about it? Get angry? Seek vengeance? Seethe? Not Epictetus. Why? Because it was not a matter of good character. How can this be a helpful way to think about it? Because it comes down to our fundamental nature as rational beings. "So what is the divine nature?" Epictetus asks. "It is mind, intelligence and correct reason" (*Discourses*, Book II, 8, 2). We need "look no further than" reason "for the substance of the good" (*Discourses*, Book II, 8, 3), and the good is all we should care about when it comes to living in harmony with how nature made us and thus how we can live a life of virtue, which is a sufficient condition for *eudaimonia*, or human flourishing and fulfillment.

As Professor Michael Sugrue explains in a lecture about the *Meditations* of Marcus Aurelius, Epictetus the slave, and Marcus the emperor, were no different in their ability to partake of philosophy, which is accessible to all human beings. They were both capable of striving to be wise men who are disciplined and in control of their emotions, following the way of nature.

The good man, Sugrue continues, "can be a good man no matter what his position in the social structure is."[48] As Julia Annas writes: "As rational beings interacting as members of a community of rational beings, owner and slave realize that the barriers between them are completely conventional. Whether someone is a slave is a matter of fortune, and does not affect his ability to become virtuous, to live as well in the conditions of his life as a free person does in his."[49]

Moreover, since he is not responsible for the social structure, he should not be distressed by his position in this structure. As Sugrue explains, if the gods of nature make you a slave, then be a good slave. If they make you an emperor, then be a good emperor. "Your job is not to disgrace yourself. Live up to the highest potential of human beings," which, we might add, may involve advocating for the abolition of slavery (justice) while simultaneously trying to live a virtuous life while you are a slave.

On the latter note, we should add, as the British philosopher Julia Annas writes, that "to moderns what stands out is that the Stoics never recommend trying to abolish or even reform the institution of slavery itself; they limit their recommendations to acting within it." Yet coming back to the point about constrained optimization, we must also add that "ancient slavery was profoundly embedded in every aspect of society," and "it was not open to a slave-owner, as it was later to an American slave-owner in the South, to free his slaves and adopt another approach."[50]

Thus, a "would-be reformer would have been silenced, either by ridicule or literally." Thus: "It is the circumstances of ancient society that limit the ways Stoics could act with regard to slavery, not the limitations of thinking in terms of virtue."[51] In any case, Annas continues, it was on appeal to virtue that abolitionist activism would succeed in ending slavery in the late eighteenth- and nineteenth-century Britain.

One key point about virtue is that human happiness is a matter of personal responsibility. God made man, says Epictetus, and "of all his creatures, [man] alone [was] given the power of self-determination" (*Discourses*, Book II, 8, 21). God "entrusted you to yourself, saying, 'I had no one more dependable than you; just see that he keeps the qualities he was born with: integrity, honor, dignity, patience, calmness and poise'" (*Discourses*, Book II, 8, 23). Despite all the constraints imposed by society and nature, your well-being depends ultimately on you and how you make the best use of what you have (i.e., reason). As stated by the Roman orator Cicero: "unless the mind be in a sound state . . . there can be no end of our miseries."[52]

This emphasis on personal responsibility stands in contrast with the emphasis of Critical Social Justice that well-being in society is less fundamentally a function of personal autonomy or responsibility than it is a function of the group by which one is classified, explicitly or implicitly, ideologically or discursively, in society. However, Critical Social Justice is also not unaligned with Stoicism, which has a strong streak of communitarianism. Indeed, in talking about Stoicism and social utility at Stoicon 2018, Professor Long reminds us that Marcus Aurelius regularly reminded himself that "we are born for community," while Epictetus claimed that "we are so constituted that we can attain none of our own goods unless we contribute something to the common interest."[53]

As noted, it would have been perfectly consistent for Epictetus to focus on living virtuously as a slave while advocating for the abolition of slavery. The point is to not let your soul fall into chaos as a result of things outside your control. Being a slave may not be under your control but deciding to advocate for abolition of slavery is. You can be oppressed as a slave but be content in always trying to do the right thing. Similarly, you can be oppressed by the responsibilities of being an emperor surrounded by intrigue, plague, and war but be content in knowing you always tried to do the right thing.

Given the centrality of Logos and our immanence in nature, this communitarianism is a necessary implication. "If what philosophers say about the kinship of God and man is true," Epictetus said, "then the only logical step is to do as Socrates did, never replying to the question of where he was from with, 'I am Athenian,' or 'I am from Corinth,' but always, 'I am a citizen of the world'" (*Discourses*, Book I, 9, 1).

How does this cosmopolitanism work? When we know "how the whole universe is administered," we know "that the first, all-inclusive state is the government composed of God and man." This government is "the source of the seeds of being, descending upon his father, his father's father—to every creature born and bred on earth, in fact, but to rational beings in particular, since they alone are entitled by nature to govern alongside God, by virtue of being connected with him through reason." Reason makes us "citizens of the world and children of God" (*Discourses*, Book I, 9, 4–6).

As a communitarian philosophy, Professor Long notes,[54] Stoics don't aim at converting the world to Stoicism, but at benefiting their constituents in ways that are conducive to people's mental and physical welfare. Thus, Stoics can advocate for improving public health care, for example, on the grounds that it is good for the community. It is in harmony with our nature as rational beings for whom justice is one of the four cardinal virtues. How to square this with the view that we should be "indifferent" to health and wealth, even if it is okay to prefer them to sickness and poverty? It is not that health and wealth are not desirable. They are certainly to be preferred over poverty and sickness. We regard health and wealth as indifferent *with respect to virtue*.

Citing the Stoic philosopher Antipater, Long explains that we should work relentlessly to obtain the things that accord with nature. We can do this by cultivating virtue, not pursued for one's *own virtuous sake*—rather, for *the sake of virtue itself*. "From the point of view of happiness," Dirk Baltzly explains, "the things according to nature are still indifferent. What matters for our happiness is whether we select them rationally and, as it turns out, this means selecting them in accordance with the virtuous way of regarding them (and virtuous action itself)."[55]

One might say it is not about congratulating oneself for embracing virtue, but congratulating virtue when one embraces it. As a citizen of the world,

Epictetus explained, "a person never acts in his own interest or thinks of himself alone, but, like a hand or foot that had sense and realized its place in the natural order, all its actions and desires aim at nothing except contributing to the common good" (*Discourses*, Book II, 10, 4). It is then up to each person, as Long notes, to make the best of himself given his real-life situation and his own individuality.[56]

We also should not have much trouble seeing that dedication to virtue, or excellence of character, demands dedication to justice in the sense of fairness for all groups in society. As Kai Whiting and Leonidas Konstantakos write in *Being Better*: "In Stoicism, virtue includes speaking up against injustice and greed."[57] Justice, like wisdom, is one of the four principal virtues of Stoicism, but we might say that wisdom is prior to justice because it is wisdom that must be cultivated if reason is to perceive what must be done to achieve justice. This is not exactly right because, for the Stoics, all the virtues are interconnected, and neither is separate from the other as prior or posterior. The point is that wisdom is knowing how and when to follow truth wherever it leads. The challenge, of course, is how to find the right path—the one that leads to the truth.

None of this is necessarily inconsistent with Critical Social Justice or Critical Theory. For example, in his essay "Traditional and Critical Theory," Max Horkheimer describes "critical thinking" as:

> the function neither of the isolated individual nor of a sum-total of individuals. Its subject is rather a definite individual in his real relation to other individuals and groups, in his conflict with a particular class, and, finally, in the resultant web of relationships with the social totality and with nature.[58]

But there is a fundamental difference between Stoicism and Critical Social Justice. For Critical Social Justice, it comes down to the examination of institutions that socialize us into our roles. Turning inward to cultivate one's virtue and character, with an eye toward gearing your actions so that they stem from good intentions, is not likely to be enough to change the world. To use terms from contemporary discourse on social justice, it is *impact*, not *intent*, that matters most. You *do* have control over externals such as power and privilege. You should turn outward to transform society to minimize the harmful impacts it can have on your physical and mental health.

Again, this emphasis is not inconsistent with Stoicism in the sense that an inevitable consequence of reason guiding us toward virtue is that we want to turn outward and contribute to the improvement of society for the benefit of our fellow humans. Donald Robertson sums up this cosmopolitanism in *How to Think Like a Roman Emperor*:

In addition to believing that humans are essentially thinking creatures *capable of reason*, the Stoics also believed that human nature is inherently *social*. They started from the premise that under normal conditions we typically have a bond of "natural affection" toward our children. . . . This bond of natural affection also tends to extend to other loved ones, such as spouses, parents, siblings, and close friends. The Stoics believed that as we mature in wisdom we increasingly identify with our own capacity for reason, but we also begin to identify with others insofar as *they're* capable of reason.

In other words, the wise man extends moral consideration to all rational creatures and views them, in a sense, as his brothers and sisters. That's why the Stoics described their ideas as *cosmopolitanism*, or being "citizens of the universe"—a phrase attributed both to Socrates and Diogenes the Cynic. Stoic ethics involves cultivating this natural affection toward other people in accord with virtues like justice, fairness, and kindness. Although this social dimension of Stoicism is often overlooked today, it's one of the main themes of *The Meditations*. Marcus touches on topics such as the virtues of justice and kindness, natural affection, the brotherhood of man, and ethical cosmopolitanism on virtually every page.[59]

The implicit claim of Critical Social Justice, however, is that virtue resides fundamentally in institutions (externals) rather than in ourselves. It is true that society is made up of the citizens of which it is comprised, so we cannot reform society without reforming ourselves, and so in an important sense, virtue does ultimately reside in ourselves. Moreover, critical theorists like the Frankfurt School philosophers believed deeply in the promise of human autonomy. The difference is that one finds in the ideas of Critical Social Justice a conception of human nature as malleable, crucially shaped by the historical circumstances in which it lives, rather than in the natural order of the Logos.

Institutions are not only buildings, schools, and museums, but norms and habits we internalize as members of society. For Critical Social Justice, social reengineering is about reengineering our malleable natures because it is the unwitting *impact* our socialized behaviors have on others that matters, not the cultivation of virtuous *intent* that can lead to positive impact on others.

Critical Social Justice is more pessimistic than Stoicism about the inherent capacity for human beings, as creatures endowed by nature with reason, to enact change by cultivating their capacity for virtue. Critical Social Justice is primarily (though not exclusively) a *consequentialist* philosophy rooted in *critique* of institutions, whereas Stoicism is a *eudaimonistic* philosophy rooted in cultivation of virtue, and like humanism, encourages *criticism* of ourselves and of institutions. Critical Social Justice focuses on impact, while Stoicism steers our attention to intent. For Stoicism, virtue convinces us to be motivated to advance justice and improve society. Critical Social Justice is skeptical of the notion that one's intent can always be trusted; impact is what matters, and impact flows fundamentally from social relations based on power and privilege.

NOTES

1. Diogenes Laertius, *Lives of the Eminent Philosophers*, p. 252.

2. Kai Whiting and Leonidas Konstantakos, *Being Better*, p. 1.

3. St. George Stock, *A Guide to Stoicism* audiobook (12:45), https://www.youtube.com/watch?v=xlUE3WxZjiM.

4. Stoicism, Internet Encyclopedia of Philosophy, https://iep.utm.edu/stoicism/.

5. Tony Long, "Stoicism Ancient and Modern," Stoicon 2018 (45:00), https://www.youtube.com/watch?v=_xuQ4i46K_M&t=7s.

6. Donald Robertson, "Introduction to Stoicism: The Three Disciplines," February 20, 2013, https://donaldrobertson.name/2013/02/20/introduction-to-stoicism-the-three-disciplines/.

7. Stoicism, Stanford Encyclopedia of Philosophy, first published Monday April 15, 1996; substantive revision Tuesday April 10, 2018, https://plato.stanford.edu/entries/stoicism/.

8. Tony Long, "Stoicism Ancient and Modern," Stoicon 2018 (15:00), https://www.youtube.com/watch?v=_xuQ4i46K_M&t=7s.

9. Donald Robertson, *How to Think Like a Roman Emperor*, p. 30.

10. Stoicism, Internet Encyclopedia of Philosophy, https://iep.utm.edu/stoicism/.

10. Stoicism, Internet Encyclopedia of Philosophy, https://iep.utm.edu/stoicism/.

11. Diogenes Laertius, *Lives of the Eminent Philosophers*, pp. 252–253.

12. Diogenes Laertius, *Lives of the Eminent Philosophers*, p. 253.

13. Diogenes Laertius, *Lives of the Eminent Philosophers*, pp. 268–270.

14. A History of Philosophy: Stoicism, by Arthur Holmes, https://www.youtube.com/watch?v=xLJNaLGK5Aw.

15. Stoicism, Internet Encyclopedia of Philosophy, https://iep.utm.edu/stoicism/.

16. Massimo Pigliucci and Gregory Lopez, *A Handbook for New Stoics: How to Thrive in a World Out of Your Control* (New York: The Experiment, 2019), audiobook (26:50): https://www.youtube.com/watch?v=-McaP887yYo. Stoicism, Internet Encyclopedia of Philosophy, https://iep.utm.edu/stoicism/.

17. Tony Long, "Stoicism Ancient and Modern," Stoicon 2018, 31:00, https://www.youtube.com/watch?v=_xuQ4i46K_M&t=7s.

18. Diogenes Laertius, *Lives of the Eminent Philosophers*, p. 261.

19. David E. Hahm, *The Origins of Stoic Cosmology* (Ohio State University Press, 1977), p. 3.

20. Margaret R. Graver, *Stoicism and Emotion*, pp. 19–20.

21. Margaret R. Graver, *Stoicism and Emotion*, p. 20.

22. Margaret R. Graver, *Stoicism and Emotion*, p. 19.

23. Margaret R. Graver, *Stoicism and Emotion*, p. 19.

24. Stoicism, Stanford Encyclopedia of Philosophy, first published Monday April 15, 1996; substantive revision Tuesday April 10, 2018, https://plato.stanford.edu/entries/stoicism/. David E. Hahm, *The Origins of Stoic Cosmology* (Ohio State University Press, 1977), chapter 2.

25. Stoicism, Stanford Encyclopedia of Philosophy, first published Monday April 15, 1996; substantive revision Tuesday April 10, 2018, https://plato.stanford.edu/entries/stoicism/.

26. A History of Philosophy: Stoicism, by Arthur Holmes, https://www.youtube.com/watch?v=xLJNaLGK5Aw (30:30).

27. A History of Philosophy: Stoicism, by Arthur Holmes, https://www.youtube.com/watch?v=xLJNaLGK5Aw (31:20).

28. A History of Philosophy: Stoicism, by Arthur Holmes, https://www.youtube.com/watch?v=xLJNaLGK5Aw (31:20).

29. A History of Philosophy: Stoicism, by Arthur Holmes, https://www.youtube.com/watch?v=xLJNaLGK5Aw (33:00).

30. A History of Philosophy: Stoicism, by Arthur Holmes, https://www.youtube.com/watch?v=xLJNaLGK5Aw (33:30).

31. A History of Philosophy: Stoicism, by Arthur Holmes, https://www.youtube.com/watch?v=xLJNaLGK5Aw (35:00).

32. Pierre Hadot, *The Inner Citadel*, chapter 5.

33. Pierre Hadot, *The Inner Citadel*, p. 83.

34. Donald Robertson, "Introduction to Stoicism: The Three Disciplines," February 20, 2013, https://donaldrobertson.name/2013/02/20/introduction-to-stoicism-the-three-disciplines/.

35. Pierre Hadot, *The Inner Citadel*, pp. 185, 187.

36. Pierre Hadot, *The Inner Citadel*, p. 189.

37. Pierre Hadot, *The Inner Citadel*, p. 101.

38. Donald Robertson, "Introduction to Stoicism: The Three Disciplines," February 20, 2013, https://donaldrobertson.name/2013/02/20/introduction-to-stoicism-the-three-disciplines/.

39. Donald Robertson, *How to Think Like a Roman Emperor*, p. 167.

40. Ryan Holiday and Stephen Hanselman, *Lives of the Stoics*, p. 172.

41. Tony Long, "Stoicism Ancient and Modern," Stoicon 2018 (32:40), https://www.youtube.com/watch?v=_xuQ4i46K_M&t=7s.

42. Tony Long, "Stoicism Ancient and Modern," Stoicon 2018 (45:55), https://www.youtube.com/watch?v=_xuQ4i46K_M&t=7s.

43. Pierre Hadot, *The Inner Citadel*, p. 74.

44. Pierre Hadot, *The Inner Citadel*, p. 74.

45. Kai Whiting and Leonidas Konstantakos, *Being Better*, p. 47.

46. Kai Whiting and Leonidas Konstantakos, *Being Better*, p. 47.

47. Michael Sugrue, Marcus Aurelius: Lecture on Stoicism (full lecture) (9:00): https://www.youtube.com/watch?v=L5_an6B3H4E.

48. Julia Annas, *Intelligent Virtue*, p. 59.

49. Julia Annas, *Intelligent Virtue*, p. 60.

50. Julia Annas, *Intelligent Virtue*, p. 60.

51. Cicero, *Tusculan Disputations*, translated by C. D. Yonge, p. 54, Book III, Section VI.

52. Tony Long, "Stoicism Ancient and Modern," Stoicon 2018 (36:50), https://www.youtube.com/watch?v=_xuQ4i46K_M&t=7s.

53. Tony Long, "Stoicism Ancient and Modern," Stoicon 2018 (38:00), https://www.youtube.com/watch?v=_xuQ4i46K_M&t=7s.

54. Stoicism, Stanford Encyclopedia of Philosophy, first published Monday April 15, 1996; substantive revision Tuesday April 10, 2018, https://plato.stanford.edu/entries/stoicism/.

55. Tony Long, "Stoicism Ancient and Modern," Stoicon 2018 (14:30), https://www.youtube.com/watch?v=_xuQ4i46K_M&t=7s.

56. Kai Whiting and Leonidas Konstantakos, *Being Better*, p. 24.

57. Max Horkheimer, *Critical Theory: Selected Essays*, pp. 210–211.

58. Donald Robertson, *How to Think Like a Roman Emperor*, pp. 40–41.

Chapter 4

What Does Stoicism Have to Say
about Social Justice Activism?

The worldview of Critical Social Justice is not without insight. It is not hard to see that society can be stratified in ways that confer ongoing benefits to some groups at the expense of other groups.

The question is what to do about it.

Chapter 2 described how Critical Social Justice conceives of oppression and marginalization, as well as its paradigm for how to think about changing society. Reform is not unwelcome, but Critical Social Justice is about kindling a revolution. It has in mind a radical reshaping of prevailing institutions because they purportedly, and irredeemably, underlie a set of norms, habits, beliefs, and attitudes that will perpetuate inequalities among social groups if we do not undertake efforts to rethink, disrupt, and restructure society.

In seeking to change norms, habits, beliefs, and attitudes, it is with an eye toward reengineering society as a way of reengineering ourselves as human beings. It is an attempt to use the power of institutional forces to make us better people rather than encouraging us to become better people to create better institutions.

Galvanized by critical theories about race, gender, class, sexual orientation, and other identities, Critical Social Justice activism is anchored on a politics of identity that relies on the framework of intersectionality (the basic idea that all oppression is interconnected within a system that stratifies people by social groups) to think about social justice. The idea is to pick apart social hierarchies by illuminating and challenging the norms, beliefs, and attitudes that reinforce the habits by which we become "socialized" into "roles" we are expected to perform based on the groups to which we are assigned based on race, ethnicity, gender, sexual orientation, and so on. This socialization is an insidious, ideological process that assimilates us into society and necessarily makes us complicit in its injustice if we are not actively working to dismantle it.

Moreover, while grass-roots consciousness-raising is important, it is oriented toward top-down institutional change. A core belief, in the words of Karl Marx, is that "it is not consciousness of men that determines their being, but, on the contrary, their social being that determines their consciousness."[1] This is not a beneficial state of affairs if, as the late philosophy professor Rick Roderick once claimed, Marx was "right . . . that as far as the history of ideas go, the ruling ideas in each epoch are basically the ideas of the ruling classes, the dominant ones. Not all the ideas, but the dominant ideas of each historical period will be the ideas discussed by the dominant classes."[2]

In this view, ideologies produced by systems of power—racism, sexism, and (for Marx) capitalism—indoctrinate people with ideas that undergird exploitative power relations between races, sexes, or classes within society. To borrow from Noam Chomsky and Edward S. Herman, it is a system of "manufacturing consent."[3] As Frankfurt School affiliate Erich Fromm points out, "Marx gave a fuller statement with regard to the problem of consciousness in German Ideology":

> The fact is, therefore, that definite individuals who are productively active in a definite way enter into these definite social and political relations. Empirical observations must in each separate instance bring out empirically, and without any mystification and speculation, the connection of the social and political structure with production. The social structure and the State are continually evolving out of the life-process of definite individuals, but of individuals, not as they may appear in their own or other people's imagination, but as they really are; as they are effective, produce materially, and are active under definite material limits, presuppositions and conditions independent of their will.[4]

Half a century after Marx died, the Italian neo-Marxist Antonio Gramsci took up a similar task. A highly influential thinker in the philosophy and praxis of education, Gramsci proposed an ideological battle for hearts and minds conducted by partisan "organic" intellectuals who acquire positions of influence within the institutional apparatus of "civil society" in which culture is reproduced. While Gramsci's target was capitalism, he pinned the blame for exploitation on "cultural hegemony."

For Gramsci, like other western Marxists, capitalism is an exploitative system that thrives on the consent of the exploited. Consent is manufactured via ideology, a set of ideas that lead to norms of culture, particularly within civil institutions like schools and churches. While "political society" protects the ruling class and preserves the status quo by using the coercive apparatus of laws, courts, police, prisons, and the military, "civil society" protects the ruling class and preserves the status quo by producing the cultural institutions by which subaltern classes internalize the cultural norms that reinforce the status quo, effectively manufacturing their consent.

Gramsci advocates a "war of position," in which organic intellectuals work within the culture to transform the culture. As explained in a paper by Valeriano Ramos Jr., "the creation of the new organic ideology is effectuated dialectically through 'ideological struggle': the aspiring hegemonic class adopts an articulating principle that makes it possible to absorb, rearticulate, and assimilate ideological elements in the discourse of other social classes, and to unify these elements into a new collective will."[5]

Gramscian neo-Marxism is a precursor to social justice activism in its call for political agitation and a revolutionary "war of position" in which the aim is to gain control of the means of (cultural) production. In a postmodern world where truth is regarded as inseparable from localized contexts, a similar line of thinking has been taken up by scholars and activists schooled in Critical Theory (especially the philosophy and praxis of education, or Critical Pedagogy) to advocate for change and constructing a society deemed more favorable to a revolutionary world view.

This is not a conspiratorial matter involving cabals of "critical theorists" meeting in dark rooms to talk about how to take power and purge the "ruling class" by sending them to the proverbial gulag. It is, however, a matter of Critical Social Justice becoming an intellectual ethos in the university and in other cultural institutions in society, a trend that can be traced to the legacy of Marx, Gramsci, and the Frankfurt School, among many others.

The aim, in the words of Horkheimer, is the "possibility of a wider vision, not the kind possessed by industrial magnates who know the world market and direct whole states from behind the scenes, but the kind possessed by university professors, middle-level civil servants, doctors, lawyers, and so forth . . . what constitutes the 'intelligentsia,' that is, a special social or even supra-social stratum."[6]

Take, for example, an article in *The New York Times*, in which Professor Jason Barker celebrates the birthday of Karl Marx:

> The key factor in Marx's intellectual legacy in our present-day society is not "philosophy" but "critique," or what he described in 1843 as "the ruthless criticism of all that exists: ruthless both in the sense of not being afraid of the results it arrives at and in the sense of being just as little afraid of conflict with the powers that be." "The philosophers have only interpreted the world, in various ways; the point is to change it," he wrote in 1845.

Professor Barker connects this "critique" to the modern social justice movement:

Racial and sexual oppression have been added to the dynamic of class exploitation. Social justice movements like Black Lives Matter and #MeToo owe something of an unspoken debt to Marx through their unapologetic targeting of the "eternal truths" of our age. Such movements recognize, as did Marx, that the ideas that rule every society are those of its ruling class and that overturning those ideas is fundamental to true revolutionary progress.[7]

Similarly, social commentator Bradly Mason has noted: "both CLS [critical legal studies] and CRT [critical race theory] scholars saw themselves as working within the 'Critical Marxist' tradition of György Lukács, Karl Korsch, and the Frankfurt School, as opposed to the 'Scientific Marxist' tradition of the Communists."[8] Queer theorist Judith Butler writes on behalf of herself and her coauthors Ernesto Laclau and Slavoj Žižek in *Contingency, Hegemony, Universality: Contemporary Dialogues on the Left*, "we have all, I believe, worked at the theoretical margins of a Left political project, and have varying degrees of continuing affinity with Marxism as a critical social theory and movement."[9]

This trend reached a culmination in the 2010s, as noted in the discussion of Jonathan Haidt and Greg Lukianoff's *The Coddling of the American Mind* in chapter 2. Jordan Peterson picked up on these themes when lumping them into what he called, somewhat amorphously, "postmodern neo-Marxism" after coming to fame in 2016 when he recorded videos on YouTube attacking an act passed by the Canadian Parliament. The act was designed to prevent discrimination by gender but, he argued, would unjustifiably force the use of gender pronouns in violation of free speech. Peterson connected this legislation to the prevalence of identity politics and political correctness in modern society, attributing their origins to ideas from the academy.

Peterson faced fierce criticism from many quarters, in part by conflating Marxism and postmodern philosophy while granting postmodern philosophers more political clout than they probably deserve. The criticism was not unwarranted, as exhibited, for example, in a debate with renowned philosopher Slavoj Žižek in which Peterson appeared to have a superficial grasp of the substance of Marx's voluminous writings.

Peterson may not be as deeply immersed in the history of these ideas as he is in his field of academic expertise, but he was not incorrect in identifying the long shadow of Marx's influence on generations of intellectuals and political activists that culminated in the Critical Theory of the Frankfurt School, as well as the activism of the 1960s and 1970s that followed. In turn, this activism—explored in books such as *SDS* by Kirkpatrick Sale, *Days of Rage* by Bryan Burroughs, and *The Critical Turn in Education* by Isaac Gottesman[10]—contained the seeds of a decades-long effort by radical activists to take refuge in the university and assume positions from which to pass on their strain of progressive activism to a new generation of students.

As Gottesman writes, this was already well underway in the early 1990s:

> "To the question: 'Where did all the sixties radicals go?', the most accurate answer," noted Paul Buhle (1991) in his classic *Marxism in the United States*, "would be: neither to religious cults nor yuppiedom, but to the classroom." After the fall of the New Left arose a new left, an Academic Left. For many of these young scholars, Marxist thought, and particularly what some refer to as Western Marxism or neo-Marxism, and what I will refer to as the critical Marxist tradition, was an intellectual anchor.[11]

As noted above, Marx wrote that "the social structure and the State are continually evolving out of the life-process of definite individuals, but of individuals, not as they may appear in their own or other people's imagination, but as they really are; as they are effective, produce materially, and are active under definite material limits, presuppositions and conditions independent of their will.[1213] This is a key tenet of Critical Social Justice: individuals cannot reach their full potential, or achieve autonomy, without eradicating the social conditions that preserve a ruling class at the expense of the alienation of individuals within the subaltern class, or what Marx called the proletariat.

In contrast, the Stoics believed that human potential begins with the individual's will. Endowed by nature with the faculty of reason, the individual has the capacity for autonomously making decisions that are in harmony with nature (Logos). As Epictetus insisted, "reason is unique among the faculties assigned to us in being able to evaluate itself—what it is, what it is capable of, how valuable it is—in addition to passing judgment on others" (*Discourses*, Book I, 1, 4).

This does not imply that the Stoic individual is born to be Robinson Crusoe. Not at all. As Pierre Hadot writes: "Intelligence and reason are common to all reasonable beings; hence they are universal. This is why they are that common and universal law which is within all rational beings, for by virtue of their universality which transcends individuals, they allow us to shift from the egocentric viewpoint of the individual to the universal perspective of the All." Thus, "self-preservation and self-coherence are possible only by virtue of complete adherence to the Whole of which one is a part."[14]

Stoicism is about the fundamental capacity of the individual to use his faculty of reason to develop his character so that it is rooted in the four cardinal virtues: wisdom, courage, justice, moderation. These four interconnected virtues are themselves related to the idea that we are inseparable from the community of other human beings who make up the society in which we live. "To be a Stoic," Hadot writes, "means to become aware of the fact that no being is alone, but that we are part of a Whole made up of the totality of rational beings and that totality which is the Cosmos."[15]

Stoicism and Critical Social Justice share a fundamental interest in improving social conditions so that human beings can achieve their potential. But while Stoicism puts trust in individuals as creatures of reason who can assent to correct assessments of the reality around them, Critical Social Justice starts with society and is inclined to see reason as potentially compromised in its ability to form correct assessments of reality. Consider an example from critical race theory, a branch of critical theory.

Gary Peller, a professor of constitutional law at Georgetown University Law Center and contributor to and coeditor of *Critical Race Theory: The Key Writings that Formed the Movement*, writes that critical race theorists "began to explore how liberal categories of reason and neutrality themselves might bear the marks of history and struggle, including racial and other forms of social power." For example, a post-Civil Rights increase in the matriculation of Black students "into mainstream institutions wasn't enough to achieve racial equality—because once inside the gates, they confronted norms organizing what was taught and how it was taught that had been created exclusively by Whites operating in all-White institutions. There were, or could be, racial power dynamics embedded even in what was called 'knowledge' in academia or 'neutrality' in law."[16]

Moreover, while both Stoicism and Critical Social Justice are interested in improving social conditions for the benefit of everyone, Stoicism has a more cosmopolitan, virtue-based vision for social justice than Critical Social Justice, whereas the latter is more pessimistic about the ability of human beings to pursue social justice on the basis of virtue without consideration of the benefits (what Stoics called "externals") that they can ensure for themselves.

As an example, a core tenet of critical race theory is "interest convergence," which is the idea that many, if not most, White people are only interested in policies or practices that help improve the socioeconomic status of Black people if there is a corresponding benefit to White people. Critical race theory is skeptical of the idea that enough White people can get on board with reforms to help Black people to tip the societal scales.[17] This skepticism may help explain the critique of "Whiteness" that one finds in the works of writers and scholars as far back as W. E. B. Du Bois, Frantz Fanon, and James Baldwin.

One prominent field closely related to critical race theory is critical Whiteness studies. This field sees "Whiteness" as a central pillar of a racially stratified society and focuses less on widening the circle of inclusion in society and more on deconstructing and decentering "Whiteness." Whiteness, according to pioneering scholar Ruth Frankenberg, is (1) "a location of structural advantage, of race privilege"; (2) "'a standpoint,'" a place from which White people look at themselves, at others, and at society"; and (3) "a set of cultural practices that are usually unmarked and unnamed."[18]

Robin DiAngelo, an influential public figure and former scholar in critical Whiteness studies, who became famous for her best-selling book *White Fragility*, describes Whiteness as follows:

> Whiteness is thus conceptualized as a constellation of processes and practices rather than as a discrete entity (i.e., skin color alone). Whiteness is dynamic, relational, and operating at all times and on myriad levels. These processes and practices include basic rights, values, beliefs, perspectives and experiences purported to be commonly shared by all but which are actually only consistently afforded to white people. Whiteness Studies begin with the premise that racism and white privilege exist in both traditional and modern forms, and rather than work to prove its existence, work to reveal it.[19]

This conceptualization of Whiteness might run into problems with Stoics if only because of its logically fallacious formulation. One: It begs the question by assuming the conclusion in its premise (rather than working to prove existence, it assumes privilege in any given situation and works to reveal it). Two: It succumbs to the reification fallacy, according to which an abstraction such as "Whiteness" is assumed to take on material existence in the form of White people living their daily lives. In other words, it tends to anthropomorphize "Whiteness" by seeing it as taking on a life of its own within society.

The reification fallacy can mislead us into having distorted, or one-dimensional, views of reality, such as reading great works of literature as mere political tracts that illuminate what is ultimately a logical fallacy— the reification of Whiteness. For example, reading *Narrative of the Life of Frederick Douglass* as simply a polemical diary or political narrative in an effort to "decenter" Whiteness can obscure the masterfully composed intellectual maturation of a former slave despite the nearly insurmountable challenges of being a Black man in a profoundly racist nineteenth-century American society.

It can mislead us into thinking that "white silence is enabling American racism."[20] Or that White dietitians who endorse the Mediterranean diet are upholding White supremacy.[21] Or that diversity training should teach us about "being less White."[22] Or that teachers should tell students that White people cannot experience racism.[23] Or that Whiteness manifests in grocery stores with ethnic food aisles.[24] Or that shampoo can teach us about White privilege.[25] Or that all White people are racist.[26]

All this aside, Critical Social Justice mainly conflicts with Stoicism in its conception of "individualism" and "universalism" as discursive practices embedded in our language that prevent us from reaching our potential as autonomous beings endowed with reason. In her PhD dissertation, DiAngelo argued that "individualism and universalism" are "two master discourses of Whiteness in practice." According to DiAngelo, individualism "posits that Whites are first and foremost individuals who have earned their place in society on their own merit," which "works to deny that Whites benefit from their racial group memberships." The other so-called discourse, universalism, "posits that White interests and perspectives are objective and representative of all groups."[27]

Individualism and universalism, along with what DiAngelo calls a discourse of personal experience, "serve to obscure White power and privilege and to reproduce Whiteness." Her dissertation is dedicated to discussing "the implications of these findings for teacher education, classroom teaching, and for White researchers conducting race related research."[28] As argued in an essay on the "Orwellian dystopia of Robin DiAngelo's PhD dissertation,"[29] DiAngelo's educational praxis leans heavily on speech monitoring and indoctrination.

Moreover, in contrast to the Socratic dialogues that inspired the ancient Stoics, it takes on a view more akin to that of the ancient sophist Protagorus, who claimed that "man is the measure of all things," which Plato interpreted as a denial of objective truth. Indeed, DiAngelo has insisted that "there is no objective, neutral reality."[30]

DiAngelo is only one among many scholars in the field of critical Whiteness studies. But her work and her rise to fame with the publication of *White Fragility* has put critical Whiteness studies at the forefront of an increasingly bitter divide between supporters and opponents of critical race theory. The book *Reinventing Racism: Why "White Fragility" Is the Wrong Way to Think about Racism*, presents a comprehensive critique of DiAngelo's theory of White fragility. But this should not be taken to mean that there is no merit in critical Whiteness studies, or more broadly, in the controversial field of critical race theory.

In the remainder of this chapter, we explore how Stoicism can help us navigate the bitter controversies that have emerged about some of the key claims of this incipient field of critical Whiteness studies, and perhaps bring to light both the merits and demerits of a focus on "decentering Whiteness." This notion has become increasingly influential in the Gramscian project of initiating a "war of position," particularly in the academy, to revolutionize and reengineer the way we think about social justice, and more specifically in this chapter, about racial justice.

As one example, sociologists Tukufu Zuberi and Eduardo Bonilla-Silva, in their book *White Logic, White Methods* on how social science methodology can sustain racism, write that they "hope the readers who find the book useful use it as ammunition in the *war of position* against the manifestations of White supremacy in the social sciences."[31] On the face of it, this hope is quite innocuous. What reasonable person can object to eradicating White supremacy? The issue, however, is not only their reference to Gramsci's project, but in how they understand White supremacy. This directs our attention to the meaning and significance of "Whiteness" in contemporary scholarship that falls under the umbrella of critical Whiteness studies, and more broadly, Critical Social Justice.

WHITENESS AND RACIAL JUSTICE

In July 2020, the Smithsonian National Museum of African American History and Culture posted a chart on its website titled "Aspects & Assumptions of Whiteness & White Culture in the United States." As part of its attempt to get readers "talking about race," it described White dominant culture, or *Whiteness*, as referring "to the ways White people and their traditions, attitudes, and ways of life have been normalized over time and are now considered standard practices in the United States."[32] Listed among the presumed aspects and assumptions of Whiteness were individualism; objective, rational linear thinking; and the notion that "hard work is the key to success."[33]

The chart proved controversial. Within days, the reaction proved so swift and influential that the museum decided to remove the chart and issue an apology. Declaring that "it is important for us as a country to talk about race," the museum thanked "those who shared concerns about our 'Talking About Race' online portal." The museum highlighted the importance of "frank and respectful interchanges as we as a country grapple with how we talk about race and its impact on our lives."[34] The museum admitted it was in error, removed the chart from the portal, and apologized.

The museum's decision to remove the chart was commendable, not simply because it was problematic to imply that rational thinking and hard work are the exclusive domain of "White" culture (or people), thus failing to "provide increased understanding" as hoped, but because it was the result of having "listened to public sentiment" and deciding the chart "does not contribute to the productive discussion we had intended." Adhering to its mission "as an educational institution," the museum stressed that it values "meaningful dialogue and believe[s] that we are stronger when we can pause, listen, and reflect—even when it challenges us to reconsider our approach."[35]

The museum deserves credit for being receptive to critique, just as it deserves credit for stimulating conversations about the challenges that society confronts in overcoming racism while promoting diversity and inclusion. The museum ran into trouble by taking its cue from critical Whiteness studies,

mechanically and unartfully drawing from concerns about the limits of rationality and the Protestant work ethic, in centering Whiteness as "the core of
understanding race in America."[36]

This is not to say it is unreasonable to intimate how "the normalization
of White racial identity throughout America's history [has] created a culture
where nonwhite persons are seen as inferior or abnormal."[37] But the concept
of Whiteness can be deeply problematic, if only because what marks the
norms and habits that distinguish American culture as uniquely "White" is
subject to ambiguity and misdirection.

Moreover, one must contend with the distinction between norms adopted
as part of a culture in which Whites are the majority and norms adopted
for a majority specifically because they are "White" norms. For example,
it seems reasonable to assume that flesh-colored Band-Aids tend to have a
lighter color because the majority of people in American and European societies are White, not because lighter skin is necessarily associated with White
supremacy.

Nevertheless, to the extent that Whiteness refers, as described by the portal,
"to the way that White people, their customs, culture, and beliefs operate as
the standard by which all other groups of [sic] are compared," the museum
is correct to put "Whiteness" at "the core of understanding race in America."
Indeed, "this White-dominant culture . . . operates as a social mechanism that
grants advantages to white people, since they can navigate society both by
feeling normal and being viewed as normal." In other words, "persons who
identify as White rarely have to think about their racial identity because they
live within a culture where Whiteness has been normalized."[38]

As mentioned in the section above, the notion of "whiteness" in critical
whiteness studies fall preys to the reification fallacy (treating an abstraction
as if it has a material existence), but what concerns us is the ambiguity that
surrounds whiteness, like a fog that obscures legitimate disagreements about
whether, as the portal states, "Whiteness (and its accepted normality) also
exist as everyday microaggressions toward people of color."[39] The issue of
microaggressions is only one example, but an important one given concerns
in the psychological literature about the robustness of the research that underlies it; and as discussed in chapter 2, concerns about "fragility" activism.

The notion of whiteness as it applies to day-to-day contemporary life may
be ambiguous, but ambiguity by itself is by no means a basis for closing off
discussions about "whiteness" as it relates to race in America. It may instead
stimulate efforts to confront ambiguity and get a solid grasp of what whiteness entails. If anything, it is not unreasonable to reflect on the nature and
implications of white privilege, taking caution, as in the case of whiteness, to
do so as rigorously as possible.

The museum was thus not without cause in urging readers to reflect on how "being white does not mean you haven't experienced hardships or oppression" but does mean that "you have not faced hardships or oppression based on the color of your skin."[40] Nonetheless, the racial reckoning in America to which the museum seeks to contribute must come to terms with the ambiguity of whiteness.

If it does not, the conversation on race risks becoming dogmatic. It risks making everything about whiteness if it fails to clearly delineate the contours of what constitutes "white" space, allowing every possible grievance to osmotically diffuse into the conversation about what whiteness is and how it applies to daily life. This is akin to whiteness scholar Robin DiAngelo insisting, "the question is not 'Did racism take place?' but rather, 'In which ways did racism manifest in this specific context?'"[41]

When the boundaries are so blurred around such a sensitive topic, it does not bode well for careful, calm, and scrupulous dialogue. This is unfortunate because serious dialogue about race, whiteness, and diversity is sorely needed in America. As Timothy Carney, resident fellow at the American Enterprise Institute, wrote in an op-ed about the controversy that arose about the chart on the Smithsonian museum's online portal, "we should understand that cultural values are a real thing and that in a multicultural society, you'll end up with at least subtly clashing values."[42]

For example, Carney continued, "the [museum's] poster parallels the arguments pushed by some leading writers on race," referencing a *New York Times* report on an anti-racist seminar in which the instructor "expounded that white culture is obsessed with 'mechanical time'—clock time—and punishes students for lateness." In other words, Carney wrote facetiously, "being on time is white now."

Carney expresses "no doubt that different cultures have different ideas of what's 'on time,'" and recounts how he and his wife "once attended [his] cousin's wedding in Puerto Rico," which started "about 45 minutes late, and most of the guests seemed totally unfazed by that." Concluding the point, Carney notes that "a surprising number of formal studies have shown how much culture determines one's perception of time." The Protestant work ethic, presumably one of the targets of the controversial graphic, arguably has contributed to an obsession with "being on time."

Nevertheless, the museum's decision was the right one if only because sweeping racial generalizations are unhelpful. Are "objective, rational linear thinking" and the claim that "hard work is the key to success" illustrations of "being white"? It is not hard to see how such generalization may imply there is something inherently "white" (rather than Stoic) about rationality and hard work. It is also not hard to see how such racial essentialism can undermine the mission of anti-racism.

More unfortunate, however, is that in the fractious society in which we live, the museum's apology may have gone unnoticed as an exemplary stake in the narrowing grounds of reconciliation between competing camps on how to "talk about race." The apology revealed a refreshing willingness to consider critique without rejecting it out of hand and should have been received by detractors not with smug self-satisfaction, but with gratitude. It also might have provided critics with an opportunity to reciprocate by grappling with the exclusionary impacts of "whiteness."

In short, the entire affair began as an attempt to illustrate how aspects and assumptions of whiteness are important to address when we "talk about race," but in the aftermath of the controversy that ensued, may have provided an example of the kind of reasoned reconciliation that can arise from even-handed engagement with critique. The museum's action stands in respectable contrast to the obstinacy and partisan rancor that often stymie conversations about race and racial inequality.

THE STOIC PERSPECTIVE

In the *Meditations*, Marcus Aurelius wrote, "remember that to change your opinion and to follow him who corrects your error is as consistent with freedom as it is to persist in your error" (*Meditations*, Book 8). In the *Enchiridion*, Epictetus, wrote that "[you must cultivate either your own reason or else externals; apply yourself either to things within or without you—that is, be either a philosopher or one of the mob" (*Enchiridion*, XXIX).

A question arises: as a Stoic, should one rely on one's own reason and judgment, or defer to the reason and judgment of others? The answer: it depends. For the Stoics, one of the four principal virtues one should cultivate in life is wisdom. Diogenes Laertius described what the Stoics understood as wisdom: "knowledge of things good and bad and of things neither good nor bad."[43] For example, it could entail knowledge of what constitutes racial injustice and how to correct it.

How to acquire wisdom? As we learned in earlier chapters, the key is to cultivate reason. "Our main strength," Epictetus writes, "[should] be applied to our reason" (*Enchiridion*, XLI). For Stoics, reason stands at the center of both the universe and human action. It is reason that allows us to gain the kind of healthy perspective about our affairs that can helpfully guide our decisions and actions, especially with respect to applying the four cardinal virtues in our lives. But one must do so with diligence and determination.

As Donald Robertson explains at length in *How to Think Like a Roman Emperor*, the nurturing of reason and virtue was a long and arduous journey for Marcus Aurelius, no less than a Roman emperor, and did not come without a great deal of training under the guidance of mentors like Junius Rusticus. In the *Meditations*, the emperor wrote: "From Rusticus I received the impression that my character required improvement and discipline; and from him I learned not to be led astray by emulating others" (*Meditations*, Book 1).[44] We rely on others to arrive at a point at which we can rely on ourselves.

Even at maturity, wisdom does not imply solipsism or self-isolation. We are, after all, interconnected with the world around us—nature, institutions, and other people. As Marcus wrote in the *Meditations*, we should "frequently consider the connection of all things in the universe and their relation to one another. For in a manner all things are implicated with one another, and all in this way are friendly to one another; for one thing comes in order after another, and this is by virtue of the active movement and mutual cohesion and unity of the substance."[45]

Stoicism strongly encourages us to figure out how we fit within the order of nature and society, learning to accept what we cannot control and act upon what we can control. Part of this task may involve learning not only when one must rely on one's own reason, but when one must seek advice from others.

One could say the pursuit of wisdom is an art and a science. With wisdom, one is well-prepared to balance confidence in one's own reason against the humility to acknowledge when a friend or gadfly correctly discerns our errors based on the exercise of his own reason. We can see the Smithsonian museum's decision to take down the chart on whiteness as an example of this balancing act.

The remainder of this chapter explores another example of the societal conversation on whiteness, how it has proved controversial, and how a Stoic might try to provide advice on how to handle the complexities involved. It provides the kind of measured approach a Stoic might take in trying to understand whiteness in the attempt to promote a more racially harmonious society.

CASE STUDY: *BREAKING BAD* AND WHITENESS STUDIES

A few years ago, there was a story in the *Guardian* about the decision by acclaimed poet Claudia Rankine to donate her $625,000 MacArthur "genius grant" to establish the Racial Imaginary Institute.[46]

The purpose of the institute was to study whiteness. In her interview with the *Guardian*, she talked about how the concept of whiteness seems foreign to people. For example, she found herself unable to find books on whiteness in a bookstore at the Los Angeles Contemporary Museum of Art. When she went to ask for help, the salesclerk looked puzzled and came up empty.

In her interview, she explained her interest in the "conceptions and constructions of whiteness" and in understanding "what makes whiteness, or about how broad the life experiences of white people are." In her attempt to elaborate, Ms. Rankine did not appear to be as open-minded about the broad experiences of white people as she was in how those experiences undergird white dominance.

For example, while people are supposedly inclined to associate Blackness with criminality, she described how shocked people are when she informs them about a women's prison in Ohio in which 80 percent of the women are white rural women, as if it could not be possible that only 19 percent of the women are Black. This is apparently a part of "white America that we don't see in the media," with the notable exception, she claims, of the Emmy award-winning show *Breaking Bad*.

Even then, she claims, "the only way that whiteness equals criminality" is when "a dying white guy" breaks the law "so he could take care of his family." This remark is a telling slip that indicates an underlying presumption that whiteness is inextricable from white supremacy. This suggests an angle underlying the purpose of the Institute that could introduce bias into its scholarly objective—namely, not to unpack all the ways in which being white may or may not contribute to white supremacy, but only the ways in which being white does contribute to white supremacy.

This proclivity for confirmation bias (the tendency to believe what you want to believe about how to interpret a given situation, ignoring evidence that may conflict with your interpretation) becomes immediately apparent when she discusses a remark by the novelist Jonathan Franzen that he does not write about race because he does not "have very many black friends" and has "never been in love with a black woman."[47]

It is an "embarrassing confession," he admits, and one that prompts Ms. Rankine to ask: "So, why don't you know these people? What choices have you made in your life to keep yourself segregated? How is it one is able to move through life with a level of sameness? Is that conscious? Is segregation forever really at the bottom of everything? When he says something like that, I find that really interesting as an admittance to white privilege: that he can get through his life without any meaningful interaction with people of color."

One interesting aspect of her questions is the implicit catch-22 embedded in them. Anyone paying attention to the discourse about whiteness invariably comes across some version of the view that "having Black friends" does not insulate you from racism. Nor does it mean that you have a license to write a novel about Black people—or that if you do, it will authentically represent the "lived experiences" of Black people (one reason publishers are increasingly reluctant to publish novels about the experiences of a protagonist from a specific social group if the author is not also a member of the same social group[48]). In other words, having Black friends does not mean you can understand what it means when you read stories about "napping while Black," "driving while Black," "shopping while Black," "moving while Black," or in general, "existing while Black."

At the same time, however, when Franzen gingerly expresses regret about not having many Black friends, he is faulted for having lived a segregated life, as if he were an instantiation of the unavoidable reality that systems are in place to lure him into a segregated life. Moreover, Ms. Rankine perceives this segregation as an admission of white privilege, even though Mr. Franzen seems quite open to cultivating relationships with people of color, if only because he expresses regret about not having those relationships.

It all potentially adds up to the catch-22 in which a white person may feel uncertain about what he is supposed to do, which, by the way, would apparently illustrate a core point in critical whiteness studies that white people are oblivious to the ways that whiteness is a pillar of discourse that keeps them secluded in an ideological bubble.

This is not to make us feel sympathy for white people for getting backed into a catch-22. The point is not, yet again, to reinforce and reify whiteness by failing to recognize how the "system" keeps white people oblivious to the discourses by which they keep the system in place. Rather, it is to point out that critical whiteness studies, as a niche subfield within the broad array of studies that constitute Critical Social Justice, points the finger at "externals"—in this case the institutional forces behind segregation—as the source of inertia in race relations.

This is distinct from a Stoic point of view, which places responsibility on the individual. This means that a white person acting virtuously can recognize that it is in the interest of justice to seek out relationships with people of color, and that institutional "externals" are less an impediment than a person's lack of virtue.

In *Intelligent Virtue*, Julia Annas conceives of virtue as a skill that is distinguished by the "need to learn" and the "drive to aspire."[49] The idea is not to learn the skill by rote, as if a mere matter of routine and simulation of what a teacher is showing you to do. It is instead about learning to exercise the skill by intuition, with the aim being how to do something not by rote but by self-direction: "you have to make the effort to understand what you have been taught, and to grasp it for yourself."[50]

Ms. Annas invokes the example of a "pianist whose goal is to play like Alfred Brendel, but mistakenly thinks that she will achieve this by copying all his mannerisms and niceties of style, playing only the pieces he plays and playing them just as he plays them." This is not a skill in the sense that a "person who really learns to play in a way that could be called 'playing like Brendel' might do so in playing quite different pieces, in different ways from

Brendel, but in ways that show that she has learnt about playing from Brendel and grasped what is central to his style." The person acquiring a skill is a learner with an "aspiration [that] leads the learner to strive to *improve*, to do what he is doing better rather than taking it over by rote from the teacher."[51]

"Where the aspiration to improve fails," Ms. Annas continues, "we lapse into simple repetition and routine."[52] If we think about (racial) justice as one of the cardinal virtues, the Stoic might venture to say that Mr. Franzen is acting virtuously in confronting the reality that he does not have many relationships with Black people. It is not exactly virtuous to characterize the reality as an "embarrassing confession," as the Stoics would probably refer to the descriptive term "embarrassing" as a mistake in judgment (it may feel embarrassing, but embarrassment impedes, rather than facilitates, the cultivation of virtue). Mr. Franzen should simply accept his reality and then go about cultivating more relationships with Black people. But recognizing this reality as a limitation of his writing is to recognize the reality of his situation and push him to seek out relationships with more people.

To the extent it leads him to aspire to form these relationships, we can say that he is on his way to working on the "skill" of virtue. Note that Ms. Rankine qualifies her remarks by specifying that Mr. Franzen has avoided meaningful interaction with people of color, indicating that the "skill" or "virtue" that Ms. Rankine has in mind is not superficial, but meaningful, relationships with Black people. Perhaps it is meaningful relationships that could facilitate Mr. Franzen's growth in his skill as a writer—namely, as a writer who could go on to write a novel about race as compellingly as he does about family.

In this sense, we can say that Stoicism and whiteness studies are both interested in whiteness as a "lack of skill" (lack of virtue) on the part of white people to formulate meaningful relationships with Black people and thus become more in harmony with the whole human community.

However, we also return to the basic difference that Stoicism focuses on encouraging (white) people to cultivate virtue as a skill that will facilitate a more harmonious relationship with nature and the human community, thus benefiting the human community. Scholars of whiteness studies focus instead on the structural impediments that preclude white people from exercising this virtue. One of these impediments is the "discourse" of white people who say they have Black friends without understanding that "having Black friends" does not necessarily imply that you have meaningful relationships with Black people (i.e., more than just routine acquaintances).

In either case, however, we are compelled to ask: is it a privilege to get through life without "meaningful interaction" with people of color? It does not necessarily seem the case for Mr. Franzen. It may be that he is embarrassed because he publicly confesses to self-segregation, but his sense of chagrin may also reflect a genuine wish that he could write about race. It may be that he regards never having loved a Black woman or not having "very many black friends" as a lack of privilege.

Is Mr. Franzen privileged to have gone through life without meaningful interaction with people of color? Or is meaningful interaction with people of color a privilege he has been denied? Ms. Rankine does not ask the latter question despite its relevance to what she deems a "more critical evaluation of one's own habits and one's own positionality relative to making art and doing work."

Or, she might have added, relative to cultivating virtue in the interest of racial justice. Why does she not ask the latter question? One hesitates to speculate. The focus of her comments is Mr. Franzen's segregated existence in relation to the production of his art. But it is not inconsistent with the focus of Critical Social Justice on "externals" such as institutions and systems that, rooted in history as they are, are ever present and stymie the development of human autonomy that might otherwise exercise its will and cultivate virtue. For example, critical race theory, Kimberlé Crenshaw explains, is "an approach to grappling with a history of White supremacy that rejects the belief that what's in the past is in the past and that the laws and systems that grow from that past are detached from it."[53]

Contrast this perspective with the Stoic perspective, as articulated by Pierre Hadot in *The Inner Citadel*:

> Here we must recall that, for the Stoics, the future was just as much determined as the past. For Destiny, there is neither future nor past, but everything is determined and definite. . . . Walking is "present"—that is, it belongs to me currently—when I am walking. The past and the future, by contrast, do not currently belong to me. Even if I think about them, they are independent of my initiative and do not depend on me. Therefore, the present has reality only in relation to my consciousness, thought, initiative, and freedom. It is these which give it a kind of thickness and duration, which in turn is linked to a series of unities: of the meaning of the discourse which I utter, of my moral intention, and of the intensity of my attention.[54]

The Stoics were by no means blind to the interconnections between past, present, and future. "For the Stoics," Hadot writes, "events were predicates, as we saw in the case of 'walking,' which is present to me when 'I am walking.' If, then, an event happens to me, this means that it has been produced by the universal totality of the causes that constitute the cosmos"[55] past, present, and future.

For the Stoics, however, the will acts in the present. The Stoics highlighted the central role of *prohairesis*, our will or "principal cause" according to Cicero, as one of the many causes of action in the universe. Given the activist bent of critical race theory in particular and Critical Social Justice in general, social justice scholars and activists do not disagree on the need for personal agency and action.

However, while *prohairesis* ("intent" if we are to draw from the lexicon of Critical Social Justice) is central to the Stoic view when it comes to moral responsibility for social injustice, it is history (because of its impact on the present) that is central to the view of Critical Social Justice. Why is all this important? For the Stoic, reason can and should determine how we think about things and thus exercise our will. For Rankine, like scholars and activists schooled in Critical Social justice, "culture really does determine what we think [and] how we think about things."

Consider the show *Breaking Bad*—a show about a high school chemistry teacher named Walter White who is diagnosed with terminal cancer and gets involved in illicit methamphetamine production. The plot hinges on the motives that explain why a level-headed, law-abiding family man who teaches high school chemistry gets entangled with a cartel of ruthless villains running a global meth trade.

The first few episodes demonstrate that Walt's initial motive is not, as Rankine suggests, "so he could take care of his family." Eventually, Walt does calculate the amount he believes is necessary to provide for their future long-term financial security, which includes goals such as mortgage payments and a college education for his children ($737,000). But it is not these goals that initially turn Walt's attention to meth production. It is medical expenses that accrue after he is diagnosed with terminal cancer.

It is true that his family's financial situation is still a factor because he does not want to leave his family burdened with medical debt after he dies. But Walt's medical plan will pay for his cancer treatment. It is only when his wife urges him to seek care from one of the top oncologists that medical expenses estimated at $90,000 become a factor in his decision to continue involvement in meth production (the costs balloon because the doctor is out-of-network). Even then, his wealthy friend from graduate school, Eliot Schwartz, offers to pay for his care, but Walt refuses.

Why?

When Walt refuses to take a job offer from Mr. Schwartz, which would have given him top-notch health insurance that would cover additional expenses associated with cancer treatment directed by a top oncologist, we begin to understand that deeper motives are at work. Mr. Schwartz even offers to pay for the treatment outright after Walt refuses to take the job; but Walt does not want charity from a man he believes built a billion-dollar business in part based on ideas that reflect Walt's own original work. Walt believes Eliot stole his work and made a fortune. Pride and resentment are the passions, or vices, that propel Walt on his descent into criminality.

Walt begins his career in meth production with an impulsive decision to take up an offer from his brother-in-law, a federal agent of the United States Drug Enforcement Agency who occasionally gives Walt a hard time about his boring life and invites Walt to come along on a raid one day to get some "action" in his life.

While on a raid, Walt sees an old student escape from a house. He subsequently searches out his old student, Jesse Pinkman, and coaxes Jesse into helping him make money from cooking meth. Walt naively thinks that he can cook a few premium batches and let Jesse do the dirty work of selling his premium version of meth on the streets. But Walt inadvertently stumbles into murdering a player in the local drug scene. After clumsily removing all traces of the murder, while unconvincingly trying to appease his conscience, he persuades Jesse to follow through on distributing the meth product on the streets.

This does not produce the financial windfall Walt anticipated. Disappointed, Walt sets out on a path of ad hoc ventures that culminate in a lucrative alliance with a drug kingpin named Gus Fring, who controls the trade all over the southwest of the U.S. Gradually, frictions arise between him and Gus, which complicate his relationship with Jesse and other players in the industry. The result is a chain of complex, ad hoc decisions, each of which reflects a separate cost-benefit analysis, but each of which also immerses him more deeply and irredeemably in the business of drugs, murder, and money laundering.

This brings us to the central point. Walt is an underachieving high school chemistry teacher with a PhD-level understanding of chemistry. He sold his interest in a company that went on to become a billion-dollar enterprise; and now spends his days teaching apathetic high school students, feeling humiliated when those students see him working a second job at a car wash. He has a loving family, but also harbors resentments about having sold his interest in a fledgling company to a man who would make billions off his research. It doesn't help that the same man married the woman Walt was in once in love with.

Death can bring a man face-to-face with all the regrets of his life. How Walt deals with regret is the central theme of the show. The Stoics viewed regret like they did emotions in general: as products of value judgments that can have harmful consequences for one's long-term well-being if one forms mistaken judgments that result in negative emotions like regret. Such a course does not help one get onto the path of *eudaimonia*. It constitutes a failure to come to terms with one's experiences as being interconnected with the Logos of the universe. As noted above, the Stoics believed that events were predicates. "If, then, an event happens to me, this means that it has been produced by the universal totality of the causes that constitute the cosmos."

For the Stoic, in the words of Ryan Holiday, "the obstacle is the way." It is the choices one makes in the present, in the presence of an adversity like cancer (or, say, the sting of pride that comes with accepting a gift from an old friend who has become wealthy on the basis of an idea you came up with) that determine one's virtue. This is the case whether one is acting in a morally good way or a morally bad way. But with each incremental step in his descent into moral chaos—his murders, his underworld alliances—Walt inches closer to a perverse kind of quixotic redemption for the "wrongs" he feels life has inflicted on him. In the process, he destroys his own character and threatens the well-being of his family.

Once he learns that he has the talent and poise to be a masterful criminal, he loses his grasp of virtue. He tells his wife in the series finale: "I did it for me. I liked it. I was good at it. And . . . I was . . . really . . . I was alive." This sums up a man whose innate talents found an outlet—talents that ended up being malicious and destructive. *Breaking Bad* is a tragedy of Shakespearean proportions, about a man presented with insidious opportunities to "right" the "wrongs" of his past; but, in reality, he turns fate into a series of decisions stemming from emotions (pride and resentment) that reflect morally mistaken value judgments. He ends up in a state of utter vice, completely out of alignment with his virtuous potential as a rational human being.

Breaking Bad is about the choices of a man skilled in chemistry yet unskilled in virtue. He is not wise in rejecting his former partner's offer to pay for his medical treatment. He lacks self-control. He is not courageous because he faces down drug kingpins. And he is far from courageous when he refuses to accept an offer from his former partner that could prolong his life. (The offer also provided an opportunity to work at the company that he purportedly helped spawn, not to mention a respectable means by which to provide for his family). He certainly is not helping advance the cause of justice by producing and distributing illegal drugs that destroy lives, while committing murders and deceiving his family. Though he started out as "a dying White guy" who breaks the law "so he could take care of his family," Walt loses complete control of his reason and his virtue.

Ms. Rankine claims the show presents a more benign image of Walt's criminality, as if the show purposely tries to mitigate the association between Whiteness and criminality, when in truth the entire series is about a White man who commits inexcusably bad acts. One wonders if she even has watched the show, given how quick she is to appropriate Walt's experience in the service of an ideological point. But perhaps this is not surprising given an ideological proclivity to subsume individual experience under a conceptual framework—in this case: a framework of White dominance.

In her interview, Ms. Rankine states that she "is sensitive to the experiences of people of color in almost everything she says and writes." This is as it should be, since good writing requires the ability to internalize alternative perspectives. But given her myopic interpretation of *Breaking Bad*, she does not extend the same level of effort to understand the true motives that drove Walt on his devolution into moral disarray.

Walt's descent into criminality is the story of a modern Macbeth, not the embodiment of cultural attitudes about the relation between race and criminality. It is an example of how a defining feature of life is the singularity of events. Each life is a unique compilation of aspirations (like Walt's desire to provide financial security for his family and pay for an out-of-network oncologist), disappointments (his loss of family, Eliot's "treachery," falling out with Gus Fring, disputes with Jesse), and compromised achievements (attempting to redeem a life of underachievement by cornering the meth market). Each step along the way, a man is either acting virtuously or he is not.

Race is not the issue.

NOTES

1. Erich Fromm, "The Problem of Consciousness, Social Structure and the Use of Force," 1961, https://www.marxists.org/archive/fromm/works/1961/man/ch03.htm.

2. Rick Roderick on Epicureans, Stoics, and Skeptics (25:30): https://www.youtube.com/watch?v=F660X7XV1B0.

3. Edward S. Herman and Noam Chomsky, *Manufacturing Consent: The Political Economy of Mass Media* (New York: Pantheon Books, 1988, 2002).

4. Erich Fromm, "The Problem of Consciousness, Social Structure and the Use of Force," 1961, https://www.marxists.org/archive/fromm/works/1961/man/ch03.htm. Karl Marx and Friedrich Engels, *The German Ideology* in *Selected Writings* (Indianapolis: Hackett Publishing Company, 1994), p. 111.

5. Valeriano Ramos Jr., "The Concepts of Ideology, Hegemony, and Organic Intellectuals in Gramsci's Marxism," *Theoretical Review* No. 27, March–April 1982, https://www.marxists.org/history/erol/periodicals/theoretical-review/1982301.htm.

6. Max Horkheimer, *Critical Theory: Selected Essays*, p. 221.

7. Jason Parker, "Happy Birthday, Karl Marx. You Were Right!," *New York Times*, April 30, 2018.

8. Bradly Mason, "Is Critical Race Theory Marxist?," March 23, 2021, https://alsoacarpenter.com/2021/03/23/is-critical-race-theory-marxist/

9. Judith Butler, Ernesto Laclau, and Slavoj Žižek, *Contingency, Hegemony, Universality: Contemporary Dialogues on the Left* (London, Brooklyn: Verso, 2000), p. 11.

10. Kirkpatrick Sale, *SDS* (New York: Vintage Books, 1974). Bryan Burroughs, *Days of Rage: America's Radical Underground, the FBI, and the Forgotten Age of Revolutionary Violence* (New York: Penguin Press, 2015). Isaac Gottesman, *The Critical Turn in Education: From Marxist Critique to Poststructuralist Feminism to Critical Theories of Race* (New York, London: Routledge, 2016).

11. Erich Fromm, "The Problem of Consciousness, Social Structure and the Use of Force," 1961, https://www.marxists.org/archive/fromm/works/1961/man/ch03.

htm. Karl Marx and Friedrich Engels, *The German Ideology* (Indianapolis: Hackett Publishing Company, 1994), p. 111.

12. Pierre Hadot, *The Inner Citadel*, p. 212.

13. Pierre Hadot, *The Inner Citadel*, p. 212.

14. Gary Peller, "I've Been a Critical Race Theorist for 30 Years. Our Opponents Are Just Proving Our Point for Us," *Politico*, June 30, 2021.

15. Richard Delgado and Jean Stefancic, *Critical Race Theory: The Cutting Edge*, p. 3."

16. Ruth Frankenberg, *White Women, Race Matters: The Social Construction of Whiteness* (Minneapolis: The University of Minnesota Press, 1993), p. 1.

17. Robin DiAngelo, "White Fragility," *International Journal of Critical Pedagogy*, Vol 3 (3) (2011) p. 56.

18. John Pavlovitz, "White Silence Is Enabling American Racism," The Good Men Project, May 4, 2021.

19. "Hot Take: White Dietitians Who Endorse the Mediterranean Diet Are '[Upholding] White Supremacy'," February 18, 2021, https://twitchy.com/sarahd-313035/2021/02/18/hot-take-white-dietitians-who-endorse-the-mediterranean-diet-are-upholding-white-supremacy/.

20. Paul Bond, "After Coca-Cola Backlash, LinkedIn Removes Diversity Lesson Telling Employees to 'Be Less White'," *Newsweek*, February 23, 2021.

21. Addison Smith, "Teaching Assistant Docks Point on Conservative Student's Black Panther Essay: 'White People Cannot Experience Racism,'" *The Tennessee Star*, April 6, 2021.

22. Algernon D'Ammassa, "Whiteness at the Supermarket: Readers Respond to Criticism of 'Ethnic' Grocery Aisles," *Las Cruces Sun News*, April 18, 2021.

23. Louis Staples, "Why Halsey's Hotel Shampoo Sparked Debate about White Privilege," *Newsbreak*, May 7, 2021.

24. K. Marley, "Yes, My Dear, All White People Are Racists," *Medium*, June 6, 2020; Neil Shenvi, "Quotes from Oluo's *So You Want to Talk about Race*," https://shenviapologetics.com/quotes-from-uluos-so-you-want-to-talk-about-race/.

25. Robin DiAngelo, "Whiteness in Racial Dialogue: A Discourse Analysis," PhD dissertation, University of Washington, 2004, Abstract.

26. Robin DiAngelo, "Whiteness in Racial Dialogue: A Discourse Analysis," PhD dissertation, University of Washington, 2004, Abstract.

27. Jonathan Church, "The Orwellian Dystopia of Robin DiAngelo's PhD Dissertation," *Areo Magazine*, July 14, 2020.

28. Robin DiAngelo, "My Class Didn't Trump My Race: Using Oppression to Face Privilege," *Multicultural Perspectives*, 8 (1), p. 54.

29. *White Logic, White Methods: Racism and Methodology*, edited by Tukufu Zuberi and Eduardo Bonilla-Silva (Lanham, Boulder, New York, Toronto, Plymouth: Rowman & Littlefield, 2008), p. 23.

30. Chacour Koop, "Smithsonian Museum Apologizes for Saying Hard Work, Rational Thought Is 'White Culture,'" *Miami Herald*, July 17, 2020.

31. Marina Watts, "In Smithsonian Race Guidelines, Rational Thinking and Hard Work Are White Values," *Newsweek*, July 17, 2020.

32. Chacour Koop, "Smithsonian Museum Apologizes for Saying Hard Work, Rational Thought Is 'White Culture'," *Miami Herald*, July 17, 2020.

33. Whiteness, "Talking about Race," Smithsonian National Museum of African American History and Culture, https://nmaahc.si.edu/learn/talking-about-race/topics/whiteness. These quotes have since been deleted from the site.

34. Whiteness, "Talking about Race," Smithsonian National Museum of African American History and Culture, https://nmaahc.si.edu/learn/talking-about-race/topics/whiteness.

35. Whiteness, "Talking about Race," Smithsonian National Museum of African American History and Culture, https://nmaahc.si.edu/learn/talking-about-race/topics/whiteness.

36. Whiteness, "Talking about Race," Smithsonian National Museum of African American History and Culture, https://nmaahc.si.edu/learn/talking-about-race/topics/whiteness.

37. Whiteness, "Talking about Race," Smithsonian National Museum of African American History and Culture, https://nmaahc.si.edu/learn/talking-about-race/topics/whiteness.

38. Whiteness, "Talking about Race," Smithsonian National Museum of African American History and Culture, https://nmaahc.si.edu/learn/talking-about-race/topics/whiteness.

39. Carole Schroeder and Robin DiAngelo, "Addressing Whiteness in Nursing Education: The Sociopolitical Climate Project at the University of Washington School of Nursing," *Advances in Nursing Science*, vol. 33, no. 3, p. 244.

40. Timothy P. Carney, "There's Some Truth in Those Bizarre Charts about 'Whiteness,'" *Washington Examiner*, American Enterprise Institute, July 20, 2020.

41. Diogenes Laertius, *Lives of the Eminent Philosophers*, p. 252.

42. Marcus Aurelius, *Meditations*, Book One, p. 6.

43. Marcus Aurelius, *Meditations*, 2017, Book Six, pp. 93–94.

44. Steven Thrasher, "Claudia Rankine: why I'm spending $625,000 to study whiteness," *The Guardian*, October 19, 2016.

45. Kate Samuelson, "Why Jonathan Franzen Won't Write About Race," *Time*, August 1, 2016.

46. Rebecca Christiansen, "Censorship and the Policing of Identity in Young Adult Literature," May 27, 2021.

47. Julia Annas, *Intelligent Virtue*, chapter 3.

48. Julia Annas, *Intelligent Virtue*, p. 18.

49. Julia Annas, *Intelligent Virtue*, pp. 17–18.

50. Julia Annas, *Intelligent Virtue*, p. 18.

51. Leah Asmelash, "Florida Bans Teaching Critical Race Theory in Schools," *Time*, June 10, 2021.

52. Pierre Hadot, *The Inner Citadel*, p. 136–137.

53. Pierre Hadot, *The Inner Citadel*, p. 140.

54. Steven Thrasher, "Claudia Rankine: Why I'm Spending $625,000 to Study Whiteness," *The Guardian*, October 19, 2016.

55. Pierre Hadot, *The Inner Citadel*, p. 140.

Chapter 5

Abraham Lincoln: A Stoic Model for Social Justice Leadership

Stoicism is rooted in virtue ethics. The key to a good life is to ground one's thought and action in virtue. The Stoics, not unlike other ancient philosophers, were committed to virtue as a seed that, with proper training and discipline, can blossom into the character of a person who finds peace of mind and a disposition of lasting contentment with his life (*eudaimonia*). This is achieved by harvesting the four main interconnected aspects of virtue: wisdom, courage, justice, and temperance.

One dilemma arises, however, from the Stoic idea that one is either virtuous or not. The Stoics conceive of character in absolute terms as either good or bad rather than in degrees of virtue. That is, the question is whether you are virtuous or not, not whether you are more virtuous or less virtuous today than yesterday, or more virtuous or less virtuous than another person. At the same time, they view the "Stoic sage" to be so rare that you might wonder if you can ever recognize such a person.

There is also the problem of whether the sage can recognize his own sage-hood upon attaining the disposition of one who, like a sage, makes all the right moral decisions. This dilemma recalls Meno's paradox, raised in a Platonic dialogue about virtue in which Socrates introduces the doctrine that "learning is nothing more than (the soul's) recollection."[1] This dilemma is presented to resolve the problem of how we can recognize virtue when we find it when we didn't know what it was in the first place.

As explained by *The Stoic Sage* author René Brouwer, Plutarch was keen to point out the dilemma that a Stoic sage does not know he is a sage if there is no visible point of demarcation between the successful arrival at a Stoic disposition and the conscious awareness of this arrival. We can also ask the question of whether a non-sage can ever know that he is thinking and acting as a genuinely aspiring Stoic.[2] If not, what's the point?

Brouwer offers a resolution by suggesting the interpretation that "disposition of character is . . . all that matters, on the basis of which the sage will always have a perfect grasp of the impressions." In other words, "it is the condition of mastery that counts, rather than the awareness thereof."[3] Nonetheless, the sage who is virtuous is as rare as a phoenix. So, we must ask, for all the rest of us, what are we to do? As Professor Gregory Sadler and Simon Drew discuss when they come to virtue in a podcast on the core principles of Stoicism, the Stoics wrote as if the aspiring Stoic simply needs to adopt certain thoughts and actions to live virtuously. But it is not so easy to "Just Do It," as the famous Nike slogan urges us. It takes dedication and training.[4]

For the aspiring Stoic, the pursuit of *eudaimonia* involves continuing to work on developing virtuous habits over the course of a lifetime. Given the rarity of the sage, however, the aim of reason for most of us might be said to be the pursuit of better judgment rather than perfect judgment. "The Stoics," writes René Brouwer, "followed Socrates in both attaching importance to the pursuit of striving for wisdom, and in denying for themselves perfect, divine wisdom."[5]

This means learning how to bring our thoughts and actions into alignment with nature as effectively as our own abilities and character permit. As Brouwer writes, "with regard to the change to wisdom, the cause of the change lies with oneself, that is with the development of one's reason."[6] While the acquisition of wisdom is revolutionary (i.e., you cross the line between wisdom and ignorance and you are suddenly virtuous), the process of getting there is evolutionary. Along the way, you may not be wise (virtuous), but you can strive to think and act as wisely (virtuously) as possible.

So far, this is all a matter of principle. What does this look like in practice? As Professor Sadler and Simon Drew asked in their podcast, can we think of a Stoic-like role model closer to us in time and place? Is there someone famous who strove for virtue all his life without necessarily attaining sage-hood? The ancient Stoics had Cato, Agrippinus, and Marcus Aurelius. Is there someone we can look up to today?

Surely, there are several figures in modern history who exemplify Stoic virtue to varying degrees. This chapter presents a case for Abraham Lincoln. For two reasons: (1) Lincoln steered the Union to victory in the American Civil War, resulting in the greatest advance of racial justice in the nineteenth century, while also exhibiting Stoic virtue, and (2) Lincoln has recently come under scrutiny by young social justice activists.

ABRAHAM LINCOLN: A STOIC ROLE MODEL

In *How to Be a Stoic*, Massimo Pigliucci provides a handy summary of the four aspects of Stoic virtue:

> The Stoics adopted Socrates's classification of four aspects of virtue, which they thought of as four tightly interlinked character traits: (practical) wisdom, courage, temperance, and justice. Practical wisdom allows us to make decisions that improve our *eudaimonia*, the (ethically) good life. Courage can be physical, but more broadly refers to the moral aspect—for instance, the ability to act well under challenging circumstances. . . . Temperance makes it possible for us to control our desires and actions so that we don't yield to excesses. Justice, for Socrates and the Stoics, refers not to an abstract theory of how society should be run, but rather to the practice of treating other human beings with dignity and fairness.[7]

On the last point, treating people with dignity and fairness can seem like a lost art in our era of social media trolling, populist demagogues, partisan showmanship on cable news and talk radio, and rancorous political polarization. But this is nothing new. Human affairs have been fraught with venomous conflict for centuries. Contemporary Americans do not live in a uniquely divisive society. This distinction belongs to the American Civil War when the nation was torn apart over the issue of slavery.

Bad as the Civil War was, however, America was fortunate in one crucial regard: from the ferment of conflict emerged a leader by the name of Abraham Lincoln. He was a man whose life of adversity prepared him to guide the nation to a victory that advanced the cause of racial justice more than any other event of the nineteenth century. Lincoln was no Stoic sage—something the Stoics held as an ideal rarely, if ever, to be realized in life. Nor was he a man known for abiding consciously by the principles of Stoic philosophy. This chapter suggests that Lincoln provides us with a Stoic-like model for leadership in a society that is deeply and rancorously divided by differences of thought and opinion about the nature of social justice.

This suggestion is made in the wake of recent attempts, discussed below, to "cancel" Lincoln in the name of social justice. Does Lincoln deserve to be canceled? No. Lincoln, for all his flaws, embodied the Stoics' four cardinal virtues: justice, courage, temperance, and wisdom.

While he was not without ambition, Lincoln had much in common with Cato in living a principled life, refusing to make the kind of compromises that would compromise his virtue. Though he did not commit suicide to avoid surrendering to a tyrant like Cato did, he did not let constant threats to his life stop him from pursuing the virtuous path of ending slavery and winning the

Civil War, or from going to the theater on the night that he would die at the
hands of John Wilkes Booth. One might say he effectively sacrificed his life
rather than surrender his virtue by succumbing to fear.

Lincoln was not without his share of mistakes in life. One of his "virtues"
might be that he would readily admit to not being virtuous every moment of
his life. In this respect, he was in agreement with Epictetus who said, "[i]f
anyone tells you that a certain person speaks ill of you, do not make excuses
about what is said of you, but answer: 'He was ignorant of my other faults,
else he would not have mentioned these alone'" (*Enchiridion*, XXXIII).

As Seneca says in *On Clemency*, "we are all sinners; and he that has best
purged his conscience, was brought by errors to repentance."[8] It is likely only
after a lifetime of making mistakes that Stoic sagacity is within reach. One
lives much of his life as a disciple before becoming a sage.[9] Lincoln was not
a sage, but he was a man who strived to be virtuous. In *Being Better*, Kai
Whiting and Leonidas Konstantakos write, "[l]ike a muscle, the more a person strives toward virtue, the larger and stronger they will grow and the more
effective they will become."[10]

Lincoln strived.

The aspiring Stoic strives to be virtuous. To the extent he is successful, he
confronts adversity with the kind of equanimity that not only gives him peace
of mind but facilitates his ability to contribute to the betterment of the human
community, like Lincoln leading the North to victory in the Civil War with
aplomb and without vengeance.

Lincoln had not always been so graceful under pressure, or respectful of
the dignity of others. His lifelong melancholy and episodes of debilitating
depression, particularly in the winter of 1840–41, are well-known. His humor
often came at the expense of employing racial and ethnic stereotypes.[11] He
was not immune to personal rivalries;[12] and he almost fought a duel after he
was caught foolishly maligning the reputation of a state official in satirical
articles (published under a pseudonym in a local newspaper).[13]

Like Seneca and Cicero, Lincoln was fueled by ambition and a thirst for
being in the thick of political action. But Lincoln was more like Cato in ultimately not letting an appetite for political action—and recognition among his
peers—come at the expense of cultivating his virtue. One day, after listening
to a potential client lay out his case, Lincoln concluded that the case had a
good chance of winning on a technicality, but declined to take the case. His
explanation: "Well, you have a pretty good case in technical law, but a pretty
bad one in equity and justice. You'll have to get some other fellow to win
this case for you. I couldn't do it. All the time, while talking to that jury, I'd
be thinking: 'Lincoln, you're a liar,' and I believe I should forget myself and
say it out loud."[14]

Lincoln's virtue manifested in many ways. In 1836, encouraged by mutual friends, he committed to marriage with a woman named Mary Owens despite meeting her only briefly in 1833. Upon her return to Illinois after an interval of three years spent with family in Kentucky, he regretted his decision, apparently due to her changed appearance ("I knew she was oversize, but now she appeared a fair match for Falstaff,"[15] he wrote, not so virtuously, in a letter). His reservations about marriage, his worry that he lacked an acceptable upbringing, and her criticisms of his coarse and ill-bred manners were also major issues. Yet he remained committed to his vow lest he go against his conscience.

As it turned out, she called off the engagement, maybe persuaded by his aloofness as well as his letters hinting strongly that he was not a good match. Lincoln was remiss in hastily agreeing to the marriage, but once committed, he was pained by the prospect of breaking a vow and disappointing his conscience.

In a more momentous example, the story of his reaction upon seeing enslaved Black Americans is well-known. In the words of his contemporary John Hanks: "There it was, we saw negroes chained, maltreated, whipped, and scourged. Lincoln saw it; his heart bled; said nothing much; was silent from feeling; was sad, looked bad, felt bad; was thoughtful and abstracted. I can say, knowing it, that it was on this trip that he formed his opinions of slavery. It run its iron in him then and there—May, 1831."[16]

Almost thirty-five years later, in his second inaugural address, Lincoln concluded what Frederick Douglass described as a "sacred effort" by declaring: "With malice toward none; with charity for all . . . let us strive to finish the work we are in, to bind up the nation's wounds . . . to do all which may achieve and cherish a just and lasting peace among ourselves and with all nations."[17] As the country neared the end of a civil war that had killed 620,000 men and brought an end to slavery, Lincoln sought not to inflame the passions of revenge, but to kindle a spirit of magnanimity and reconciliation.

It was no small overture. The bloodiest war in American history followed a decade of rage and recriminations over slavery that witnessed a quixotic raid on the Harper's Ferry armory that sent John Brown to the gallows, sectarian violence in Bleeding Kansas precipitated by the Kansas–Nebraska Act, the Dred Scott decision, and Charles Sumner's five-hour diatribe on the Senate floor in which he railed about the Crime against Kansas and claimed that South Carolina Senator Andrew Butler had taken a harlot (i.e., slavery) for a mistress.

Sumner's claim about Butler was a calumny against "Southern honor" so offensive to Butler's cousin, Representative Preston Brooks, that Brooks retaliated by nearly clubbing Sumner to death in the Senate chamber with a cane, as Sumner's "thighs were pinned down between his chair and his desk."[18]

Lincoln was by no means left unscathed. The years leading up to the American Civil War were fraught with a vicious partisanship that would culminate in the assassination of Lincoln at the hands of John Wilkes Booth. Upon hearing Lincoln's support for Black suffrage in a speech from a second-story window of the White House following news of Robert E. Lee's surrender, Booth turned to his coconspirator Lewis Powell in the crowd and said, "That means nigger citizenship," promising that Lincoln had given has last speech.[19] Three days later, Booth shot Lincoln in Ford's Theatre.

In the years before his assassination, Lincoln was no stranger to verbal abuse. As Mark Bowden explained in *The Atlantic*, Lincoln was repeatedly vilified: "his ancestry was routinely impugned, his lack of formal learning ridiculed, his appearance maligned, and his morality assailed." The smears came from North and South; they were recorded in "editorials, speeches, journals and private letters" and even came from ostensible allies. Both George Templeton Strong and George McClellan called him a "gorilla." Henry Ward Beecher described him as "an unshapely man." Elizabeth Cady Stanton christened him "Dishonest Abe." Charles Sumner complained that Lincoln "lacks practical talent for his important place." William P. Fessenden said he was "weak as water."[20]

Lincoln not only had to contend with public opinion. He also found himself constantly having to navigate rivalries among members of his cabinet; and even contend with treacherous insubordination by his Secretary of the Treasury, Salmon Chase. Yet Lincoln retained both his poise and his magnanimity. In the utter disarray of war, he carried on with wisdom, courage, justice, and temperance, forming the decisions, policies, and compromises that saved a nation. Like Marcus Aurelius, Lincoln was a man thoroughly engaged in world affairs without losing sight of virtue. He led a nation through a great struggle with grace and fortitude, and like Marcus, was often charitable to those who wronged him.

In *Lincoln's Melancholy*, Joshua Wolf Shenk lifts a Stoic-like phrase from a speech Lincoln gave at a state fair in Wisconsin in 1859. In the speech, immediately before farm prizes were awarded, Lincoln offered advice for the few who would win prizes and for the many who would not: "To such, let it be said, 'Lay it not too much to heart.' Let them adopt the maxim, 'Better luck next time,' and then, by renewed exertion, make that better luck for themselves." "Let it be remembered," he said, "that while occasions like the present, bring their sober and durable benefits, the exultations and mortifications of them, are but temporary; that the victor shall soon be the vanquished, if he relax in his exertion; and that the vanquished this year, may be the victor the next, in spite of all competition."

As Shenk explains, "the point of exertion was not to win a contest and then relax. Work, Lincoln suggested, was its own end, for when one worked for a proper end, neither victory nor defeat could remain; rather, both led to the need for continued effort and diligence." Lincoln then invoked the parable of an Eastern monarch "who charged his wise men to invent a sentence that would apply to all times and in all situations." The sentence: "And this too shall pass away."[21]

This is a good life lesson, as Donald Robertson notes in *How to Think Like a Roman Emperor*: "The wise man is grateful for the gifts life has given him, but he also reminds himself that they are merely on loan—everything changes and nothing lasts forever."[22] Almost like a Stoic philosopher himself, (though, again, Lincoln never called himself a Stoic), Lincoln weaves this life lesson into the grander purpose of moral progress that benefits humanity in the long term.

"How much it expresses!," Lincoln said. "How chastening in the hour of pride!—how consoling in the depths of affliction." Yet Lincoln was not satisfied. "And yet," he said, "let us hope it is not *quite* true. Let us hope, rather that by the best cultivation of the physical world, beneath and around us; and the intellectual and moral world within us, we shall secure an individual, social, and political prosperity and happiness, whose course shall be onward and upward, and which, while the earth endures, shall not pass away."[23] In other words, endurance is not mere passivity, but it is in active coordination with an enduring universe in the pursuit of justice.

In keeping with the communitarian spirit of Stoicism, Lincoln urges us to contribute to the betterment of humanity in the limited time we have. Lincoln's contributions to victory stemmed not only from a profound sympathy for his fellow human beings, but from a profound commitment to doing the right thing for its own sake.

Unlike a sage, we might add, he was not without constant agony, stress, and countless sleepless nights as he steered the nation to victory in the Civil War. But his character was that of a man who would courageously make the hard compromises necessary to preserve the Union, emancipate four million enslaved people, and foster forgiveness bestowed not by a milquetoast pushover or feckless stooge, but by a man whose inner light of virtue convinced him that redemption was more important than condemnation; and whose words of reconciliation advocated malice toward none and charity for all.

CANCELING LINCOLN?

In January 2021, the Board of Education for San Francisco, CA voted to rename forty-four public schools. According to board president Gabriela

Lopez, the vote followed a decision in 2018 to form a commission tasked with evaluating whether to rename schools as gesture to "condemn any symbols of white supremacy and racism."[24]

The commission subsequently developed criteria for determining whether to rename a school. A school would be renamed if the prominent figure whose name graced the edifice of a school building had "engaged in the subjugation and enslavement of human beings; or who oppressed women, inhibiting societal progress; or whose actions led to genocide; or who otherwise significantly diminished the opportunities of those amongst us to the right to life, liberty, and the pursuit of happiness." Among the figures included was the sixteenth President of the United States.

Abraham Lincoln was deemed to be an author of injustice.

Six months earlier, in the wake of protests over the killing of George Floyd, students at the University of Madison–Wisconsin petitioned for the removal of a statue of Abraham Lincoln on Bascom Hill. Wisconsin Black Student Union President Nalal McWhorter stated: "I just think he did, you know, some good things . . . the bad things that he's done definitely outweighs them." McWhorter was in no mood to compromise: "And I do want the 100% removal of the statue. I don't want it to be moved somewhere or anywhere like that. I want it removed."[25] In October 2020, the student government at UW–Madison passed a resolution supporting removal of the statue of Lincoln.[26]

If we claim that Lincoln is a Stoic model of virtuous leadership on behalf of social justice, then this development warrants examination. Why has Lincoln's character come under scrutiny in the annals of twenty-first-century social justice activism? Why the sudden animus toward a man whom, fifteen years after he was assassinated by John Wilkes Booth because of his role in defeating the Southern Confederacy and for authoring the Emancipation Proclamation, Frederick Douglass described as "one of the noblest, wisest, and best men I ever knew"?[27]

One reason is a main donor of the statue, Richard Lloyd Jones, "frequently published articles instigating violence against Black people," and "as owner of the Tulsa Tribune, [he] published the article that is commonly attributed with inciting the Tulsa Race Massacre of 1921."[28] Another donor was Thomas E. Brittingham Jr., "a member of UW Madison's class of 1921 Ku Klux Klan student organization."[29]

But what about Lincoln himself?

Among the reasons cited by the students at UW–Madison were that "Abraham Lincoln is a representation of ethnic cleansing of indigenous folks and the fact that UW–Madison stands on stolen land."[30] Then there is the issue of race. The Student Inclusion Coalition of UW–Madison insisted that Lincoln "was not pro-Black," labeling him instead as "anti-Black" and "anti-Native."[31] The Associated Students of Madison at UW-Madison declared that the statue of Abraham Lincoln was a remnant of the "school's history of white supremacy." In their judgment, it was necessary to remove the statue "in order to create an inclusive and safe environment for all students."[32]

Did Lincoln, famous for his attentiveness to human suffering and for authoring the Emancipation Proclamation that presaged the Thirteenth Amendment of the United States Constitution (bringing an end to slavery), actively promote ethnic cleansing? Could a man devoted to elimination of slavery since May 1831 be an outright racist who failed to promote the well-being of Black Americans? Is he someone who treated Black Americans with contempt and ill will?

Let us remind ourselves of Epictetus's advice: "Men are disturbed not by things, but by the views which they take of things" (*Enchiridion*, V). The students were reacting not to the Lincoln statue, but to an opinion they had developed about what the statue represents. The students took a view of the Lincoln statue as a remnant of the "school's history of white supremacy." They also held Lincoln personally responsible for ethnic cleaning, judged that he was "not pro-Black," and deemed it necessary to remove the statue "in order to create an inclusive and safe environment for all students."[33]

These are naive interpretations of Lincoln and his presidency. Such views take an unnecessarily myopic view of his thoughts and actions. They also lead students to mistakenly perceive a threat to their safety (and their concern for cultivating an inclusive environment on campus) based on a statue (an "external") rather than on whether the statue would threaten or undermine their ability to cultivate virtue. Perhaps the statue could stimulate honest and probing discussions about where Lincoln veered from a virtuous path. But it should not be removed. The "cancellation" campaign against Lincoln's statue was straight from the playbook of Critical Social Justice and its focus on the perceived "virtue" of an institutional monument. It also generates concern that such "fragility" activism might come at the expense of developing a more resilient, and broader, mindset.

In making this argument, however, as Lincoln would likely have done, in Stoic fashion—with malice toward none, and charity for all—that is, with an attitude of temperance and moderation, focused on the use of reason and logic to illustrate the wisdom that undergirded Lincoln's courageous pursuit of justice. As mentioned earlier, Lincoln was not immune from making mistakes. But making mistakes facilitated Lincoln's rise as a man of virtue. Lincoln was a model Stoic.

AMBITION, BUT NOT AT THE
EXPENSE OF CONSCIENCE

In the spring of 1832, war broke out between the United States and members of the Sauk, Fox, and Kickapoo tribes on land covering the present-day states of Iowa, Wisconsin, and Illinois. A Sauk named Black Hawk led this "British Band" (they brandished the British flag in defiance of U.S. sovereignty while hoping to enlist British support) east across the Mississippi River in an apparent attempt to reclaim land sold to the United States as part of the Treaty of St. Louis in 1804. Concerned about intertribal conflicts while seeking to enforce provisions of the treaty, the U.S. government sent in federal troops while state militias mobilized. Despite some early successes, Black Hawk's band was outmanned and eventually defeated within three months.

Included among the Illinois state militiamen was a twenty-three-year-old man named Abraham Lincoln. Lincoln did not end up seeing combat during the war. His participation, however, featured his first major foray into a leadership role in a formidable career that ended in his assassination after his being elected to a second term as the sixteenth president of the United States. Upon joining the militia, Lincoln was elected captain of his company, an achievement he would write about years later, saying he had "not since had any success in life which gave him so much satisfaction."[34]

Lincoln had always been an ambitious man. Of humble origins, Lincoln was, as historian Doris Kearns Goodwin explains, "conscious of his superior powers and the extraordinary reach of his mind and sensibilities . . . [and] feared from his earliest days that these qualities would never find fulfillment or bring him recognition among his fellows." At times, "when the distance between his lofty ambition and the reality of his circumstances seemed unbridgeable, he was engulfed by tremendous sadness."[35]

Lincoln lived at a time when, in words of Alexis de Tocqueville, "every American [was] eaten up with longing to rise."[36] But Lincoln aimed higher than most, telling "a colleague that he wanted to be the DeWitt Clinton of Illinois," referring to the ten-time mayor of New York City and three-time governor of New York.[37] As historian H. W. Brands notes, Lincoln's law partner William Herndon "recognized the ambition beneath Lincoln's melancholy." According to Herndon, Lincoln "was always calculating, and always planning ahead. . . . His ambition was a little engine that knew no rest." Lincoln's agony, "what oppressed his soul, was how to put that engine on the track to success."[38]

Even in the summer of 1858, after "practicing law in Springfield, Illinois, for two decades, and [achieving] most of what an able attorney could hope for in a small town in rural America," he ached for more. "Halfway into his

50th year in the summer of 1858," writes Brands, "he couldn't help wondering if his achievements would forever fall short of his dreams."[39] Beginning in August, he would embark on the first of eight famous debates with the nationally renowned Senator Stephen Douglas, gaining a reputation that would, in time, usher him to the White House, where his political star would reach its apex.

It was a long way from being a one-term Congressman in the late 1840s, failing to win renomination after unsuccessfully arguing against the Mexican American war. It was even farther away from the long and depressing winter of 1840–1841, when he broke off his engagement with Mary Owens while watching his political star fade after "internal improvements" (rails, roads, canals), which he had fervently advocated throughout the 1830s, got tied up with a state debt crisis in the wake of corruption scandals and the financial crisis of 1837. It was still farther from being elected as captain of his company in a war in which he saw no action.

Yet when all was said and done, Edwin Stanton would pronounce at his deathbed: "Now he belongs to the ages."[40] Stanton was a highly accomplished lawyer who had once dismissed Lincoln as a "long armed Ape" during a high-profile case for which Lincoln had been retained (until the case was moved from Chicago to Cincinnati and Stanton took over).[41] Stanton sang a decidedly different tune after serving as Lincoln's Secretary of War, watching Lincoln steer the nation to victory over the Confederacy, while authoring the Emancipation Proclamation and engineering its passage through Congress amidst the contingencies of war and a society marked by profound racism.

As Seneca wrote, "it is a rough road that leads to heights of greatness" (*Letter* 84). Lincoln is an illustrative case. In *Lincoln's Virtues*, William Lee Miller notes correctly that, "once Lincoln is on his own, in his early twenties, intellectually self-confident as well as amiable, personable, humorous—it is striking how rapidly his life opens out and heads upwards."[42] In *Being Better*, Kai Whiting and Leonidas Konstantakos are keen to note, "no one is an island," arguing that the "self-made man" is a myth.[43] We rely on each other as social beings. As a paradigmatic "self-made man," Lincoln's ingenuity helped, but the doors opened for him. As his star rose over the course of his career, he did not encounter the same barriers as did Frederick Douglass, former slave and acclaimed author and activist.[44]

Nonetheless, Lincoln was uniquely talented in his rise to greatness. But what are we to think of greatness? Is it about fame? Certainly not for the ancient Stoics. As Marcus Aurelius wrote, "he who has a strong desire for fame after death does not consider that every one of those who remember him will also die very soon; and also those who succeed them, until the whole remembrance shall have been extinguished as it is transmitted through men who foolishly admire and perish." Moreover, "everything which is in anyway beautiful is beautiful in itself, and terminates in itself, not having praise as part of itself. Neither worse than or better is a thing made by being praised" (*Meditations*, Book 4).

What, then, was the nature of Lincoln's ambition? Was he obsessed with contemporary or posthumous fame? It would not seem so. One clue is a famous poem on mortality by William Knox, which Lincoln memorized and recited often, and of which he once claimed: "I would give all I am worth, and go in debt, to be able to write so fine a piece as I think that is." This wistful, pensive poem asks, "Oh! why should the spirit of mortal be proud?" Recounting life's timeless rites of passages, it laments, "like a swift-fleeting meteor, a fast-flying cloud, a flash of the lightning, a break of the wave, he passeth from life to his rest in the grave." Indeed, "tis the wink of an eye—'tis the draught of a breath—from the blossom of health to the paleness of death, from the gilded saloon to the bier and the shroud:—Oh! why should the spirit of mortal be proud?"[45]

Still, Lincoln sought to rise. Just not for the sake of fame alone. While Lincoln sought recognition among his peers, he never did so at the expense of his integrity, or as a Stoic would say, at the expense of his virtue.

Consider a story about his time serving as captain of his company.[46] One day, an elderly Native American came upon Lincoln's camp. Hungry and worn down, he sought their mercy and help. The men of Lincoln's company, however, were not having it. "We have come out to fight the Indians," they averred, "and by God we intend to do it!" Desperate, the man unfurled a crumpled letter from General Lewis Cass describing him as a friend rather than enemy of the U.S. Army. The company men were skeptical, thinking the letter was a forgery and the man was a spy.

As the mob was about to pounce, Lincoln jumped in. "Men," Lincoln shouted, "this must not be done: he must not be shot and killed by us." "But," some pleaded, "the Indian is a damned spy." Aware of the dangers presented not only to the Native American but to himself, Lincoln did not relent. Someone roared: "This is cowardly on your part, Lincoln!" Lincoln held his ground. "If any man thinks I am a coward, let him test it," he said. "Lincoln," responded a new voice, "you are larger and heavier than we are." Lincoln's reply: "This you can guard against: choose your weapons."

The men relented. Lincoln won their respect for his courage and resilience. But as one source recounts, Lincoln "often declared that his life and character were both at stake, and would probably have been lost, had he not at that critical moment forgotten the officer and asserted the man." Lincoln gave to his men a demonstration of courage in defense of justice. Urging his men to cool their tempers, Lincoln would not let his captainship come at the expense of his virtue.

In exhibiting courage, Lincoln was exhibiting a virtue that not only sated his conscience, but also benefited other human beings. His action protected the Native American man from harm while saving his fellow men in the camp from committing a vice. Recall also that the virtues are interconnected with each other. In exhibiting courage, Lincoln served the cause of justice. Recall what Massimo Pigliucci wrote: "Justice, for Socrates and the Stoics, refers not to an abstract theory of how society should be run, but rather to the practice of treating other human beings with dignity and fairness."[47] Wisely urging his men to cool their tempers, Lincoln was courageously promoting temperance and defending justice.

Why did Lincoln go through so much trouble to defend the dignity and safety of the Native American? Because justice (treating other people with dignity and respect) demanded it, which helps explain how Frederick Douglass could observe that Lincoln was "the first great man that I talked with in the United States freely, who in no single instance reminded me of the difference between himself and myself, of the difference of color,"[48] and that "I was never more quickly or more completely at ease in the presence of a great man than that of Abraham Lincoln."[49]

Treating people with respect and dignity may seem like a no-brainer for a wise and virtuous citizen of the world. But Lincoln lived in a society thoroughly steeped in anti-Black racism. He probably did not entirely escape this racist worldview. Nonetheless, Lincoln's historical imagination pointed his country to a future when slavery could be eradicated, when racism could be widely understood as fundamentally unjust, and when national reconciliation was possible not only among Whites, but among everyone.

Frederick Douglass's assessment of Lincoln sheds light on a man whose virtuous character provides us with a quintessential example of a Stoic-like political leader with a talent for assimilation of ideas and actions, philosophical detachment and pragmatic activism, and faculty for parsing out the "right side of history" while navigating through a thicket of violently acrimonious political divisions in a time of war.

Throughout his career, Lincoln cultivated wisdom, demonstrated courage, advised temperance, and pursued justice. He was an ambitious man, but a man who also seemed to agree with Marcus Aurelius that "he who loves fame considers another man's activity to be his own good" (*Meditations*, Book 6). As Joshua Shenk notes, for Lincoln, "the 'larger game' was not his career but the cause of liberty."[50]

Lincoln did not let ambition get in the way of virtue. How so? By following reason. In one speech urging prudence and self-control, he exclaimed, "every son of earth shall drink in rich fruition the sorrow-quenching draughts of perfect liberty." "Happy day," he concluded, "when—all appetites controlled, all poisons subdued, all matter subjected—*mind*, all conquering *mind*, shall live and move, the monarch of the world. Glorious consummation! Hail, fall of Fury! Reign of Reason, all hail!"[51]

LINCOLN'S VIRTUE

Lincoln has come down to us through the ages as the Rail Splitter, Honest Abe, the Great Emancipator, our Greatest President. He was also a model Stoic in his commitment to a life of virtue. He was wise. He showed courage. He tempered an excess of ambition with a steadfast integrity. And he showed a moderation in his judgments that facilitated necessary compromises. Most of all, he devoted his personal and political career to the pursuit of justice.

Lincoln certainly was not pure. As a politician, he was invariably confronted with the need to make tough compromises. He was inevitably forced to consider when it was appropriate to "sell" his integrity. The question we must ask of any politician is not whether or not the politician decided to "sell" his or her integrity, but at what price he or she will "sell" that integrity. Epictetus wrote, "Consider at what price you sell your integrity; but please, for God's sake, don't sell it cheap" (*Discourses*, Book I, 2, 33). In Lincoln's case, the record is clear that he was not inclined to sell it cheap.

The Student Inclusion Coalition of UW–Madison labeled Lincoln as "anti-Black" and "anti-Native," and called for the removal of the statue because Lincoln "was not pro-Black."[52] The student coalition invoked Lincoln's fourth debate with Stephen Douglas on September 18, 1858, in which he said:

> I will say then that I am not, nor ever have been, in favor of bringing about in any way the social and political equality of the white and black races, [applause]-that I am not nor ever have been in favor of making voters or jurors of negroes, nor of qualifying them to hold office, nor to intermarry with white people; and I will say in addition to this that there is a physical difference between the white and black races which I believe will forever forbid the two races living together on terms of social and political equality. And inasmuch as they cannot so live, while they do remain together there must be the position of superior and inferior, and I as much as any other man am in favor of having the superior position assigned to the white race.[53]

On the surface, this passage appears to show Lincoln as a proponent of White supremacy. There is no mistaking the content of a passage in which Lincoln explicitly disavows "bringing about in any way the social and political equality of the white and black races." Yet are we to conclude based on this passage alone that Lincoln was racist, "not pro-Black," and in favor of White supremacy?

Decidedly, no.

In fact, to immediately jump to this conclusion would be naive and unwise. One clue appears two sentences before this passage, in which Lincoln begins his opening speech by recounting that, "while I was at the hotel to-day, an elderly gentleman called upon me to know whether I was really in favor of producing a perfect equality between the negroes and white people."[54]

This question was prompted, at least in part, by the constant race-baiting of his opponent, Stephen Douglas, who made repeated references to the "Black Republican" party in the previous debate at Jonesboro, even stoking racial anxieties with an anecdote about how Lincoln and his fellow abolitionist allies had "brought Fred Douglass to Freeport, when I was addressing a meeting there, in a carriage driven by the white owner, the negro sitting inside with the white lady and her daughter."[55]

The obvious reason for Douglas's race-baiting was that racism in American society in 1858 was deep and pervasive. When Lincoln opened his speech with a reference to the elderly gentleman's question about whether he was really in favor of racial equality, the crowd broke out in laughter, as if such a claim were ridiculous.[56] The reality is that Lincoln was already under suspicion of favoring racial equality, and Douglas relentlessly seized on this suspicion to undermine Lincoln.

In the next debate at Galesburg, Douglas not only made his own position clear when he declared: "I say to you, frankly, that in my opinion this Government was made by our fathers on the white basis. It was made by white men for the benefit of white men and their posterity forever, and was intended to be administered by white men in all time to come."[57] Douglas also insisted that Lincoln was affirming White supremacy as a matter of convenience. He referred to a speech Lincoln delivered in Chicago in July 1858 in which Lincoln said:

> I should like to know if, taking this old Declaration of Independence, which declares that all men are equal upon principle, and making exceptions to it, where will it stop? If one man says it does not mean a negro, why may not another say it does not mean another man? If the Declaration is not the truth, let us get the statue-book in which we find it and tear it out. Who is so bold as to do it? If it is not true, let us tear it out.[58]

"You find," Douglas continued, "that Mr. Lincoln there proposed that if the doctrine of the Declaration of Independence, declaring all men to be born equal, did not include the negro and put him on an equality with the white man, that we should take the statute-book and tear it out."[59] In this speech, according to Douglas, Lincoln "took the ground that the negro race is included in the Declaration of Independence as the equal of the white race, and that there could be no such thing as a distinction in the races, making one superior and the other inferior."[60] Lest there be no doubt, Douglas provides another excerpt from the speech even more explicitly supporting equality:

> My friends, I have detained you about as long as I desire to do, and I have only to say let us discard all this quibbling about this man and the other man—this race and that race and the other race being inferior, and therefore they must be placed in an inferior position, discarding our standard that we have left us. Let us discard all these things, and unite as one people throughout this land, until we shall once more stand up declaring that all men are created equal.[61]

Galesburg being in the northern region of the state, where abolitionist sentiment was more prevalent, several people in the crowd expressed support for these statements.[62] Douglas acknowledged their support but sought to make the case that this "Chicago doctrine," which Douglas called a "monstrous heresy,"[63] conflicted with Lincoln's affirmation of White supremacy in the fourth debate at Charleston, thus accusing Lincoln of inconstancy and political expediency:

> Fellow-citizens, here you find men hurrahing for Lincoln, and saying that he did right when in one part of the State he stood up for negro equality, and in another part, for political effect, discarded the doctrine, and declared that there always must be a superior and inferior race. . . . Now, how can you reconcile those two positions of Mr. Lincoln? He is to be voted for in the south as a pro-slavery man, and he is to be voted for in the north as an Abolitionist.[64]

In his reply, Lincoln clarified that his defense of political equality under the auspices of the Declaration of Independence was not a defense of social equality between the races, saying that "the judge will have it that if we do not confess that there is a sort of inequality between the white and black races that justifies us in making them slaves, we must, then, insist that there is a degree of equality that requires us to make them our wives."[65] Whatever Lincoln's "true" sentiments on race were, he clearly needed to placate the racial prejudice of his time if he had any hope of being elected. Indeed, when Douglas invoked Lincoln's affirmation of White supremacy, the crowd could be heard saying, "Good for Lincoln!"[66]

Does this mean Lincoln sold his integrity for raw ambition?

No.

As Shenk explains, we "can find common ground in Lincoln's spirit of progress. If anyone was prepared to admit his imperfections—the ones he could see and the ones he could not—it was the man himself. To pretend that all traces of racism must be scrubbed out of his life in order for him to have been a champion of progress is to create a claim that any but a perfect person must fail."[67] Similar to the Stoic sage being rare as a phoenix, it would have been impossible for a man aspiring to the presidency in 1860, even with a reputation for advocating the abolition of slavery, to be openly "pro-Black" in the manner of someone living in the twenty-first century. In fact, it would have been counterproductive.

It is true that Lincoln felt compelled to affirm white supremacy in his fourth debate with the race-baiting Stephen Douglas. It is true that Lincoln invoked racial and ethnic stereotypes in his humor. It is true that Lincoln signed the Homestead Act of 1862 and the Pacific Railway Act of 1862. It is true that Lincoln signed Morrill Act of 1862, which donated "public lands to the several States and [Territories] which may provide colleges for the benefit of agriculture and the Mechanic arts."[68] It is true that he "ordered the execution of 38 Dakota men on December 26, 1862"[69] during the Dakota War. It is also true that Lincoln was an ongoing supporter of efforts to send Black Americans to colonize Liberia, Haiti, and other parts of the war as part of his emancipation plans.

While it may seem, in all these cases, that Lincoln lacked the courage to renounce White supremacy, a Stoic perspective suggests otherwise. For the Stoic, courage is not simply about confronting adversity at all costs. As Professor Gregory Sadler explains, courage is "resisting fear for the right reason at the right time."[70] The virtues must work in tandem with each other. Courage is not courage if it is not used wisely.

If Lincoln had not affirmed White supremacy in his fourth debate with Stephen Douglas, all the eloquence of his debate performances would never have gained him the national recognition that allowed him to become president, win the war, and courageously write and sign the Emancipation Proclamation. At least since May 1831, Lincoln had been committed in his heart to the end of slavery. Moreover, Goodwin writes: "There is no way to penetrate Lincoln's personal feelings about race. There is, however, the fact that armies of scholars, meticulously investigating every aspect of his life, have failed to find a single act of racial bigotry on his part."[71]

It is also true that Lincoln pardoned not only deserters from his own Union army. He also pardoned all but thirty-eight of the more than three hundred Native American men condemned to death in the aftermath of the Dakota War, "deciding only the Dakota involved in civilian massacres should be executed."[72]

Moreover, when we take into account Lincoln's virtue, like how he treated people with dignity and respect when it truly mattered, as he did when he defended the lone Native American who fell upon his company in the Black Hawk War, Frederick Douglass seems to have come closer to Lincoln's feelings about race than the UW–Madison students when he remarked that Lincoln was "the first great man that I talked with in the United States freely, who in no single instance reminded me of the difference between himself and myself, of the difference of color."[73]

As for colonization, economic historian Phillip Magness observes that Lincoln "pitched the scheme out of a genuine concern that the post-slavery South would devolve into institutionalized racial terrorism at the hands of former plantation owners," a concern that history would eventually bear out.[74] Lincoln understood how endemic racial prejudice was in American society. He was pessimistic about the possibility of Black Americans being able to assimilate seamlessly into a White-supremacist society.

This is different from saying his colonization preference stemmed from racial animus. As Stephen Oates notes, "since the North was also a white supremacist society, most whites there were perfectly content to leave slavery alone where it already existed. Many of them may have opposed slavery in the abstract, but most rejected actual emancipation—unless accompanied by wholesale colonization—lest abolition result in a massive exodus of Southern Negroes into the North."[75]

Indeed, as Magness notes further:

While Lincoln's colonization remarks grate the modern ear, and evince a patronizing paternalism toward the program's intended participants, they also reflect the sincerity of his anti-slavery beliefs and an accompanying recognition that white-supremacist violence would not end with the formal abolition of the institution.

This condition need not be gratuitously vilified, as the 1619 Project risks doing in the absence of temperate analysis, but nor should it be obscured with misleading and mistaken historical arguments offered for the sake of discrediting a point where the 1619 Project actually has a stronger case.[76]

Lincoln recognized the deep prejudice of a society in which even Native Americans were guilty of enslaving Black Americans.[77] He genuinely believed colonization was a plausible policy that would please all sides. He was wrong and came to recognize that he was wrong when he faced criticism, particularly from Black leaders to whom he pitched his ideas. He never entirely gave up hope that it might work out, but only because he understood too well the racist society he was up against. It can be reasonably believed that he did not advocate colonization from pure racial animus.

More generally, "it is not," as William Lee Miller argues, "that [Lincoln] was, in the cliché a 'man of his time'; he was a man of his *time*, his *place*, and his *role*. He was a *politician*, a mainstream politician, seeking to shape major party victories, and much of the time seeking office himself, in one of the most racially prejudiced—perhaps the most prejudiced—of Northern states."[78]

During the controversy surrounding the Lincoln statue at UW–Madison, Nalah McWhorter explained: "I think when people say, okay, Abraham Lincoln freed the slaves. . . . I think that's looking at a very small piece of his presidency at the time. . . . So you can kind of see, here you freed the slaves, but you also did this and this and this and that."[79] This akin to saying a great baseball hitter is not great because his batting average is "only" .300 or .325. Considering Lincoln's time, place, and role, Lincoln arguably did more for social justice in the entire nineteenth century than any other person by steering the Emancipation Proclamation to passage during a time of war. If that were his only accomplishment, it arguably outweighs all other acts of his lifetime.

Of course, it was not his only accomplishment. Yet it was not his accomplishments alone that stand out for Lincoln, but the fortitude, wisdom, temperance, and justice with which he pursued them. Seneca, citing Epicurus, writes, be "as fast as [you] can, and retreat before some stronger influence comes between and takes from [you] the freedom to withdraw. But he also adds that [you] should attempt nothing except at the time when it can be attempted suitably and seasonably" (*Letter* 23). Thus, Seneca writes: "accordingly, look around you for the opportunity; if you see it, grasp it, and with all your energy and with all your strength devote yourself to that task" (*Letter* 22).

Ryan Holiday and Stephen Hanselman, writing about the Stoic philosopher Panaetius, note: "Panaetius knew that none of this philosophizing existed in a silo; it is interconnected with other important things. It is in the balance, the integrating of competing obligations and interests and talents that the good life is found and lived."[80] In his fortitude, wisdom, justice, and temperance, Lincoln showed the virtue of a Stoic-like leader who successfully navigated competing obligations, interests, and talents. In his supreme balancing act, he facilitated the greatest advance of racial justice in nineteenth-century America. In doing so, he gave us a Stoic role model for leadership on behalf of social justice.

NOTES

1. Cicero, *Tusculan Disputations*, translated by C. D. Yonge, Book I, Section XXIV, p. 18.

2. René Brouwer, *The Stoic Sage*, pp. 79–80.

3. René Brouwer, *The Stoic Sage*, pp. 84–85.

4. Gregory B. Sadler: The Core Principles of Stoicism (54:00): https://www.youtube.com/watch?v=0IITtrea0sA

5. René Brouwer, *The Stoic Sage*, p. 148.

6. René Brouwer, *The Stoic Sage*, p. 87.

7. Massimo Pigliucci, *How to Be a Stoic: Using Ancient Philosophy to Live a Modern Life* (New York: Basic Books, 2017), p. 99.

8. Lucius Seneca, *On Clemency* (Compass Circle, 2021), p. 3.

9. Liz Gloyn, "The Difference between the Stoic Sage and the Stoic Disciple," September 26, 2018, https://lizgloyn.wordpress.com/2018/09/26/the-difference-between-the-stoic-sage-and-the-stoic-disciple/.

10. Kai Whiting and Leonidas Konstantakos, *Being Better*, p. 22.

11. Joshua Wolf Shenk, *Lincoln's Melancholy* (New York: Houghton Mifflin Harcourt, 2005), p. 116.

12. *The Works of Abraham Lincoln, Vol. I, Abraham Lincoln: The True Story of a Great Life, Early Speeches 1832–1856* (New York: Newton & Cartwright; Current Literature Publishing Company, 1907), p. 59.

13. Carl Sandburg, *Abraham Lincoln: The Prairie Years and the War Years* (New York: Harcourt, Brace and Company, 1926, 1939), One-Volume Edition, pp. 76–77.

14. *The Works of Abraham Lincoln, Vol. I*, p. 97.

15. *The Works of Abraham Lincoln, Vol. IV, Letters and Telegrams, Messages to Congress, Military Orders, Autobiography, Memoranda, Etc.* (New York: Newton & Cartwright; The University Society, 1908), p. 40.

16. *The Works of Abraham Lincoln, Vol. I*, pp. 47.

17. *The Works of Abraham Lincoln, Vol. III, Abraham Lincoln: Speeches and Presidential Addresses, 1859–1865* (New York: Newton & Cartwright; Current Literature Publishing Company, 1907), p. 225. Abraham Lincoln, Second Inaugural address 1865, Saturday, March 4, 1865, http://www.let.rug.nl/usa/presidents/abraham-lincoln/second-inaugural-address-1865.php. Doris Kearns Goodwin, *Team of Rivals* (New York, London, Toronto, Sydney, New Delhi: Simon & Schuster, 2005), p. 700.

18. Speech of Honorable Charles Sumner in the Senate of the United States, 19th and 20th of May, 1856, https://www.senate.gov/artandhistory/history/resources/pdf/CrimeAgainstKSSpeech.pdf. "The Crime Against Kansas," May 19, 1856, United States Senate history, https://www.senate.gov/artandhistory/history/minute/The_Crime_Against_Kansas.htm. Daniel Lawrence Slússer, In Defense of Southern Honor: Preston Brooks and the Attack on Charles Sumner, https://digitalcommons.calpoly.edu/cgi/viewcontent.cgi?referer=http://www.google.com/url?sa=t&rct=j&q=&esrc=s&source=web&cd=1&ved=2ahUKEwjjnYPQ7oThAhUGpFkKHS3dBnkQFjAAegQIChAC&url=http%3A%2F%2Fdigitalcommons.calpoly.edu%2Fcgi%2Fviewcontent.cgi%3Farticle%3D1030%26context%3Dforum&usg=AOvVaw1HD49QoJueL9dTIHApku1a&httpsredir=1&article=1030&context=forum.

19. Doris Kearns Goodwin, *Team of Rivals*, p. 728. Joshua Wolf Shenk, *Lincoln's Melancholy*, pp. 208–209.

20. Mark Bowden, "'Idiot,' 'Yahoo,' 'Original Gorilla': How Lincoln Was Dissed in His Day," *The Atlantic*, June 2013.

21. Joshua Wolf Shenk, *Lincoln's Melancholy*, p. 157.

22. Donald Robertson, *How to Think Like a Roman Emperor*, p. 152.

23. Joshua Wolf Shenk, *Lincoln's Melancholy*, p. 157–158.

24. Bryan Pietsch, "San Francisco Scraps 44 School Names, Citing Reckoning with Racism," *New York Times*, January 27, 2021.

25. Arushi Gupta, "UW students petition to remove Abraham Lincoln statue on Bascom Hill," *Badger Herald*, June 26, 2020.

26. Jackson Walker, "UW Madison Student Government Passes Resolution Supporting Removal of Lincoln Statue," *The College Fix*, October 9, 2020. Mckenna Dallmeyer, "UW-Madison Student Gov Votes to Remove Lincoln Statue, a 'Remnant' of 'White Supremacy'," *Campus Reform*, October 27, 2020.

27. New York Historical Society, Museum & Library, https://www.nyhistory.org/exhibitions/statues-abraham-lincoln-and-frederick-douglass.

28. Arushi Gupta, "UW Students Petition to Remove Abraham Lincoln Statue on Bascom Hill," *Badger Herald*, June 26, 2020. "Reasons to Remove Abe: A History of Racism and Violence," https://twitter.com/SICofUW/status/1271845999569440768/photo/1

29. "Reasons to Remove Abe: A History of Racism and Violence," https://twitter.com/SICofUW/status/1271845999569440768/photo/1.

30. Jackson Walker, "UW Madison Student Government Passes Resolution Supporting Removal of Lincoln Statue," *College Fix*, October 9, 2020.

31. Ben Zeisloft, "UW-Madison Students Want to ancel Abraham Lincoln and . . . a Rock?," *Campus Reform*, September 22, 2020. Jonathan Turley, "'Not Pro-Black': Wisconsin Students Unanimously Vote to Remove Lincoln Statue as Racist," October 30, 2020, https://jonathanturley.org/2020/10/30/not-pro-back-wisconsin-students-unanimously-vote-to-remove-lincoln-statue-as-racist/.

32. Associated Students of Madison, University of Wisconsin-Madison, ASM Student Council, 27th Session, Legislation 27-XXXX-XX, Sponsored by: Representative Fairach, Chair George, Director Jacobson, Chair Springer, Coordinator Zhao, https://drive.google.com/file/d/1WncTd8GGgjlTb5tSloIIsosONIBUYrcP/view.

33. Associated Students of Madison, University of Wisconsin-Madison, ASM Student Council, 27th Session, Legislation 27-XXXX-XX, Sponsored by: Representative Fairach, Chair George, Director Jacobson, Chair Springer, Coordinator Zhao, https://drive.google.com/file/d/1WncTd8GGgjlTb5tSloIIsosONIBUYrcP/view.

34. Carl Sandburg, *Abraham Lincoln: The Prairie Years and the War Years*, p. 29.

35. Doris Kearns Goodwin, *Team of Rivals*, p. 102.

36. Doris Kearns Goodwin, *Team of Rivals*, p. 29.

37. Joshua Wolf Shenk, *Lincoln's Melancholy*, p. 44.

38. H. W. Brands, *Lincoln Chronicles: Dangerous Ambition*, https://www.historynet.com/lincoln-chronicles-dangerous-ambition.htm.

39. H. W. Brands, *Lincoln Chronicles: Dangerous Ambition*, https://www.historynet.com/lincoln-chronicles-dangerous-ambition.htm.

40. Doris Kearns Goodwin, *Team of Rivals*, p. 743.

41. Doris Kearns Goodwin, *Team of Rivals*, p. 174.

42. William Lee Miller, *Lincoln's Virtues* (New York: Alfred A. Knopf, 2003), p. 24.

43. Kai Whiting and Leonidas Konstantakos, *Being Better*, Chapter 5.

44. William Lee Miller, *Lincoln's Virtues*, pp. 24–25.

45. Abraham Lincoln's Favorite Poem, http://www.abrahamlincolnonline.org/lincoln/education/knox.htm.

46. Abraham Lincoln, "The Captain Faces His Men." From *The Works of Abraham Lincoln, Vol. I*, pp. 60–61.

47. Massimo Pigliucci, *How to Be a Stoic: Using Ancient Philosophy to Live a Modern Life* (New York: Basic Books, 2017), p. 99.

48. Doris Kearns Goodwin, *Team of Rivals*, p. 207.

49. William Lee Miller, *Lincoln's Virtues*, p. 41.

50. Joshua Wolf Shenk, *Lincoln's Melancholy*, p. 153.

51. Joshua Wolf Shenk, *Lincoln's Melancholy*, p. 98.

52. Ben Zeisloft, "UW-Madison Students Want to Cancel Abraham Lincoln and . . . a Rock?," *Campus Reform*, September 22, 2020, https://www.campusreform.org/?ID=15724. Jonathan Turley, "'Not Pro-Black': Wisconsin Students Unanimously Vote to Remove Lincoln Statue as Racist," October 30, 2020, https://jonathanturley.org/2020/10/30/not-pro-back-wisconsin-students-unanimously-vote-to-remove-lincoln-statue-as-racist/.

53. *The Works of Abraham Lincoln, Vol. II, Abraham Lincoln: Speeches and Debates, 1856–1859* (New York: Newton & Cartwright; Current Literature Publishing Company, 1907), p. 288. Fourth Debate: Charleston, Illinois, September 18, 1858, https://www.nps.gov/liho/learn/historyculture/debate4.htm.

54. *The Works of Abraham Lincoln, Vol. II*, p. 287. Fourth Debate: Charleston, Illinois, September 18, 1858, https://www.nps.gov/liho/learn/historyculture/debate4.htm.

55. *The Works of Abraham Lincoln, Vol. II*, p. 235, 239, 278, 282–283. The Third Debate: Jonesboro, Illinois, https://www.nps.gov/liho/learn/historyculture/debate3.htm.

56. Fourth Debate: Charleston, Illinois, September 18, 1858, https://www.nps.gov/liho/learn/historyculture/debate4.htm.

57. *The Works of Abraham Lincoln, Vol. II*, p. 47. The Lincoln–Douglas Debates, Fifth Joint Debate, Galesburg, October 7, 1858, Mr. Douglas's Speech, https://www1.cmc.edu/pages/faculty/JPitney/lincdoug.html.

58. *The Works of Abraham Lincoln, Vol. II*, p. 43.

59. *The Works of Abraham Lincoln, Vol. II*, p. 43.

60. *The Works of Abraham Lincoln, Vol. II*, p. 43.

61. *The Works of Abraham Lincoln, Vol. II*, p. 43.

62. *The Works of Abraham Lincoln, Vol. II*, p. 44.

63. *The Works of Abraham Lincoln, Vol. II*, p. 46.

64. *The Works of Abraham Lincoln, Vol. II*, pp. 44–45.

65. *The Works of Abraham Lincoln, Vol. II*, p. 53.

66. *The Works of Abraham Lincoln, Vol. II*, p. 44.

67. Joshua Wolf Shenk, *Lincoln's Melancholy*, pp. 153–154.

68. Morrill Act (1862), https://www.ourdocuments.gov/doc.php?flash=false&doc=33

69. Arushi Gupta, "UW Students Petition to Remove Abraham Lincoln Statue on Bascom Hill," *Badger Herald*, June 26, 2020.

70. Philosophy Pop-Up with Dr. Sadler-September 2017-Topic: Stoicism and "In Accordance with Nature" (10:45): https://www.youtube.com/watch?v=4LTS21ZOtxE

71. Doris Kearns Goodwin, *Team of Rivals*, p. 207.

72. University of Minnesota, College of Liberal Arts, Holocaust and Genocide Studies, US–Dakota War of 1862, "The Dakota Trials and Their Aftermath," https://cla.umn.edu/chgs/holocaust-genocide-education/resource-guides/us-dakota-war-1862.

73. Doris Kearns Goodwin, *Team of Rivals*, p. 207.

74. Phillip Magness, *The 1619 Project: A Critique* (The American Institute for Economic Research, 2020), p. 119.

75. Stephen B. Oates, *With Malice Toward None*, p. 37.

76. Phillip Magness, *The 1619 Project: A Critique*, p. 123.

77. Nicole Chavez, "Native Americans Weren't Alone on the Trail of Tears. Enslaved Africans Were, Too," CNN, May 9, 2021.

78. William Lee Miller, *Lincoln's Virtues*, pp. 354–355.

79. Arushi Gupta, "UW Students Petition to Remove Abraham Lincoln Statue on Bascom Hill," *Badger Herald*, June 26, 2020.

80. Ryan Holiday and Stephen Hanselman, *Lives of the Stoics*, p. 85.

Conclusion

In 2020, the world lived through a global pandemic amid many other challenges, while the United States witnessed mass protests, riots and looting, a soaring stock market coupled with mass unemployment, former President Donald Trump's incendiary presidential campaign and an electoral defeat he refused to concede. This all culminated in a riot on the U.S. Capitol that dragged 2020 into 2021. For this author, it was also a year marked by a storm of other calamities in his personal life.

In late January, an uncle of this author collapsed to his death in the arms of his brother, with whom he lived in the apartment they shared, after years of suffering from chronic obstructive pulmonary disease. In late February, the author's mother burned to death in a vicious house fire. In mid-March, his neurologist informed him that an MRI scan, which he had been getting on a quarterly basis since an April 2018 craniotomy to resect a brain tumor, showed an increase in tumor size and activity, requiring that he move forward with radiation and chemotherapy. Because of COVID, treatment was delayed until the summer, at which point he agreed to cease daily contact with his three-year-old daughter because regular trips to the hospital meant potential exposure to COVID.

In the face of so much adversity, what was he, or anyone else, to do? What did a Stoic mindset have to offer? One core tenet of Stoic philosophy is Epictetus's maxim that "men are disturbed not by things, but by the views which they take of things" (*Enchiridion*, V). He could have wallowed in grief and anxiety, wondering if society or the universe was waging a vendetta against him. But that would have been unhelpful, even counterproductive, like fretting incessantly about mortality.

As Epictetus tells us, "death is nothing terrible . . . but the terror consists in our notion of death, that it is terrible" (*Enchiridion*, V). There is nothing we can do about death. We are all going to die. We can exert influence on the length of our lives by exercising, eating a healthy diet, and regularly visiting the doctor. But nothing will prevent the eventual onset of mortality. Death does not discriminate. It comes to us all.

What we can control is our attitude about death. Let's look at what Marcus Aurelius had to say about posthumous fame as one potential remedy for alleviating anxiety about death: "he who has a strong desire for fame after death does not consider that every one of those who remember him will also die very soon; and also those who succeed them, until the whole remembrance shall have been extinguished as it is transmitted through men who foolishly admire and perish" (*Meditations*, Book 4).

What Marcus Aurelius is telling us is that death comes with being part of the universe, what the Stoics called Logos. Dwelling endlessly on death is to no avail. It is unavoidable. "If you wish your children and your wife and your friends to live forever," Epictetus said, "you are foolish, for you wish things to be in your power which are not so, and what belongs to others to be your own" (*Enchiridion*, XIV).

Similarly, dwelling in anxiety over the onslaught of deaths and other travesties that befell this author and the rest of the world in 2020 would have been to no avail. It is far more productive to focus on, in the words of Diogenes Laertius, "knowledge of what we ought to choose, what we ought to beware of, and what is indifferent"[1]—understanding what is within your control and what is beyond your control. When deciding upon a course of action, knowledge of what we ought to choose and what does not deserve our attention is a matter of knowing what is within one's power and what is not.

Epictetus is recorded as saying: "The chief task in life is simply this: to identify and separate matters so that I can say clearly to myself which are externals not under my control, and which have to do with the choices I actually control. Where then do I look for good and evil? Not to uncontrollable externals, but within myself to the choices that are my own."[2] How to do this? It goes back to the activation of reason in a life based on virtue—that is, based on the pursuit of wisdom, done with both moderation and courage, with an eye toward justice. In short, the good life.

Cultivating the wisdom to recognize, in any given situation, the distinction between externals not under your control and the choices you have available is also why Stoicism provides a productive way to think about social justice. It is also a viable alternative to Critical Social Justice, which came into its own during the contentious and climactic decade of the 2010s as the world climbed out of the Great Financial Crisis, dealt with the Occupy and Tea Party movements, saw a new strain of militant student activism, witnessed mass protests in Ferguson, Baltimore, and other cities, observed the election of Donald Trump as President of the United States, celebrated the legalization of gay marriage throughout the United States, and saw transgender activism go mainstream.

Critical Social Justice risks becoming an increasingly dogmatic concern with the purportedly relentless and incorrigible ways that "social constructs" preserve power and privilege. In other words, Critical Social Justice takes as its starting point the idea that human beings cannot fully achieve their potential without an uncompromising drive to revolutionize and reengineer social institutions to ensure the social conditions in which human flourishing can thrive.

The Stoics would applaud this effort to work toward the betterment of the human community. They would recognize that the institutional status quo can serve to legitimize social hierarchies. But this book argues they would object to an underlying presumption that virtue—in this case, justice—fundamentally resides in institutions rather than in ourselves.

According to the Stoics, we must cultivate our own virtue first, and everything else follows. Why? Because the life of virtue brings us into harmony with nature, which, as we may recall from chapter 1, indicates the potential within us to optimize the use of reason and to live virtuously, with each of us doing so in a way that reflects our unique individual characteristics and capabilities.

There are no virtuous institutions without virtuous human beings. As Donald Robertson writes, imagining the words of Marcus Aurelius before his death: "Man was meant to be like this: striving his whole life with patient endurance to cultivate the pure light of wisdom within himself and allowing it to shine forth for the benefit of others. Alone and yet at one with the community of fellow men around him, living wisely and in concord with them."[3]

Of course, we cannot ignore that the development of one's character takes place in interplay with a set of environmental influences. In her book *Stoicism and Emotion*, Margaret Graver writes about how Hera and Athena respond differently to the provocations of Zeus. The lesson we might glean is eminently Stoic: a person who gets angry about the social circumstances in which she finds herself cannot entirely place the blame for her anger on those circumstances.

Presumably there is something about Hera herself that explains this difference, some disposition to respond in this way that belongs to her over a long enough time that one would want to call it a trait of character.

Individual responsibility for emotions is thus bound up with the history of a person's intellectual development. In order to explain why powerful and sometimes destructive responses often seem to arise in us of their own accord, one has to appeal to a long succession of causes that have operated on a person over time. These will necessarily include such external factors as early upbringing, education, and cultural influences, as well as prior emotional experience.[4]

But "for the Stoics as for Aristotle, such causes can be identified without obscuring the contribution each individual makes to his or her own emotional formation."[5] This goes similarly for how one forms judgments about the nature of social justice. The advance of social justice depends most fundamentally not on the "externals" of institutional norms, beliefs, values, and habits, but with the individual taking responsibility for the cultivation of virtue. Why? Because while the vicissitudes of life that arise within an institutional context can take away your health, your wealth, your family, your friends, and your possessions, nothing and no one can take away your ability to choose virtue over vice.

In choosing virtue over vice, we may not be able to eliminate all the adversities that beset us, but we can be well on our way to *eudaimonia.* That is, we are on our way to being better human beings, not only on behalf of ourselves but on behalf of others, each of us making our contributions, however big or small, to forming a world with less and less adversity for current and future generations.

NOTES

1. *Daily Stoic*, The Highest Good: An Introduction To The 4 Stoic Virtues, citing Diogenes Laertius, *Lives of the Eminent Philosophers*. https://dailystoic.com/4-stoic-virtues/#:~:text=In%20Diogenes%20La%C3%ABrtius'%20Lives%20of,%2C%20 and%20what%20is%20indifferent.%E2%80%9D.

2. *Daily Stoic*, The Highest Good: An Introduction To The 4 Stoic Virtues: https:// dailystoic.com/4-stoic-virtues/#:~:text=In%20Diogenes%20La%C3%ABrtius'%20 Lives%20of,%2C%20and%20what%20is%20indifferent.%E2%80%9D.

3. Donald Robertson, *How to Think Like a Roman Emperor*, p. 266.

4. Margaret R. Graver, *Stoicism and Emotion*, p. 6.

5. Margaret R. Graver, *Stoicism and Emotion*, p. 6.

Selected References

Annas, Julia. *Intelligent Virtue* (Oxford: Oxford University Press, 2011).

Anthony Long on Epictetus and Socrates: https://www.youtube.com/watch?v=HzZyT_kHl84

Aurelius, Marcus. *Meditations,* adapted for the contemporary reader by James Harris, 2017.

Bloom, Allan. *The Closing of the American Mind* (New York: Simon & Schuster, 1987).

Bowman, Curtis. "Odysseus and the Siren Call of Reason: The Frankfurt School Critique of Enlightenment," *Other Voices, The (e) Journal of Cultural Criticism*, v. 1 n. 1, March 1997.

Brouwer, René. *The Stoic Sage: The Early Stoics on Wisdom, Sagehood, and Socrates* (Cambridge, New York: Cambridge University Press, 2014).

Church, Jonathan. *Reinventing Racism: Why 'White Fragility' Is the Wrong Way to Think about Racism* (Lanham, MD: Rowman & Littlefield, 2020).

Cicero. *Tusculan Disputations*, translated by C. D. Yonge.

Crenshaw, Kimberlé. "Demarginalizing the Intersection of Race and Sex: A Black Feminist Critique of Antidiscrimination Doctrine, Feminist Theory and Antiracist Politics," University of Chicago Legal Forum, Volume 1989, Issue 1, Article 8, https://chicagounbound.uchicago.edu/cgi/viewcontent.cgi?article=1052&context=uclf

Delgado, Richard, and Jean Stefancic. *Critical Race Theory: An Introduction* (New York: New York University Press, 2017).

DiAngelo, Robin. *White Fragility: Why It's So Hard for White People to Talk about Racism* (Boston, MA: Beacon Press, 2018).

Epictetus. *Discourses and Selected Writings* (New York, London, Toronto, Dublin, Camberwall, New Delhi, North Shore, Rosebank: Penguin Group, 2008).

———. *The Enchiridion* (Macmillan Publishing Company: New York, 1955; Bobbs-Merrill Company, Inc.: 1948).

Frankenberg, Ruth. *White Women, Race Matters: The Social Construction of Whiteness* (Minneapolis: University of Minnesota Press, 1993).

Freire, Paulo. *Pedagogy of the Oppressed* (New York: Bloomsbury Publishing, 1970).

Fromm, Erich. "The Problem of Consciousness, Social Structure and the Use of Force," 1961, https://www.marxists.org/archive/fromm/works/1961/man/ch03.htm

Goodwin, Doris Kearns. *Team of Rivals* (New York, London, Toronto, Sydney, New Delhi: Simon & Schuster, 2005).

Gottesman, Isaac. *The Critical Turn in Education: From Marxist Critique to Poststructuralist Feminism to Critical Theories of Race* (New York: Routledge, 2016).

Gramsci, Antonio. *Prison Notebooks* (London: Electric Book Company, 1999).

Graver, Margaret R. *Stoicism and Emotion* (Chicago and London: The University of Chicago Press, 2007).

Hadot, Pierre. *The Inner Citadel: The Meditations of Marcus Aurelius* (Cambridge, London: Harvard University Press, 1998).

Haidt, Jonathan, and Greg Lukianoff. *The Coddling of the American Mind* (New York: Penguin, 2018).

Hahm, David E. *The Origins of Stoic Cosmology* (Ohio State University Press, 1977).

Holiday, Ryan. *The Obstacle Is the Way: The Timeless Art of Turning Trials into Triumph* (New York: Penguin, 2014).

Holiday, Ryan, and Stephen Hanselman. *Lives of the Stoics* (New York: Penguin, 2020).

Holmes, Arthur. Lecture on Stoicism, https://www.youtube.com/watch?v=xLJNaLGK5Aw.

Horkheimer, Max. *Critical Theory: Selected Essays* (New York: Continuum, 1999).

———. *Eclipse of Reason* (New York: Oxford University Press, 1947; New York: Continuum, 1974).

Horkheimer, Max, and Theodor W. Adorno. *Dialectic of Enlightenment* (New York: Continuum, 1998).

Kellner, Douglas, and Tyson Lewis. "Liberal Humanism and the European Critical Tradition," https://pages.gseis.ucla.edu/faculty/kellner/essays/libhumanism.pdf.

Laertius, Diogenes. *Lives of the Eminent Philosophers* (New York: Oxford University Press, 2018).

Long, Anthony. "Stoicism Ancient and Modern," Stoicon 2018, https://www.youtube.com/watch?v=_xuQ4i46K_M&t=7s.

Marable, Manning. "Beyond Racial Identity Politics: Towards a Liberation Theory for Multicultural Democracy," chapter in *Privileging Positions: The Sites of Asian American Studies*, edited by Gary Y. Okihiro et al. (Washington State University Board of Regents, 1995). Reprinted in Richard Delgado and Jean Stefancic, *Critical Race Theory: The Cutting Edge* (Philadelphia: Temple University Press, 2013).

Marcuse, Herbert. "Repressive Tolerance," from Robert Paul Wolff, Barrington Moore, Jr., and Herbert Marcuse, *A Critique of Pure Tolerance* (Boston: Beacon Press, 1969), https://www.marcuse.org/herbert/publications/1960s/1965-repressive-tolerance-fulltext.html.

———. *Eros and Civilization: A Philosophical Inquiry into Freud* (Boston: Beacon Press, 1974).

———. *One-Dimensional Man* (Boston: Beacon Press, 1964).

Marx, Karl, and Friedrich Engels. *The German Ideology* (Indianapolis: Hackett Publishing Company, 1994).

Mason, Bradly. "Is Critical Race Theory Marxist?," March 23, 2021, https://alsoacarpenter.com/2021/03/23/is-critical-race-theory-marxist/.

McManus, Matthew. "What Is Critical Theory?," *Arc Digital,* April 30, 2021.

Miller, William Lee. *Lincoln's Virtues* (New York: Alfred A. Knopf, 2003).

Minnicino, Michael. "The New Dark Age: The Frankfurt School and 'Political Correctness,'" The Schiller Institute, *Fidelio Magazine*, Winter 1992.

Oates, Stephen B. *With Malice Toward None* (New York: HarperCollins, 1977).

Parker, Jason. "Happy Birthday, Karl Marx. You Were Right!," *New York Times*, April 30, 2018.

Pigliucci, Massimo, and Gregory Lopez. *A Handbook for New Stoics: How to Thrive in a World Out of Your Control* (New York: The Experiment LLC, 2019), Part 1 of Audiobook: https://www.youtube.com/watch?v=-McaP887yYo.

———. "Free Speech and Virtue Ethics," *Areo Magazine*, May 20, 2021.

———. *How to Be a Stoic* (New York: Basic Books, 2017).

Pluckrose, Helen, and James Lindsay. *Cynical Theories: How Activist Scholarship Made Everything about Race, Gender, and Identity—and Why This Harms Everybody* (Durham, NC: Pitchstone, 2020).

Ramos, Jr., Valeriano. "The Concepts of Ideology, Hegemony, and Organic Intellectuals in Gramsci's Marxism," *Theoretical Review* No. 27, March–April 1982, https://www.marxists.org/history/erol/periodicals/theoretical-review/1982301.htm.

Robertson, Donald. *The Philosophy of Cognitive-Behavioural Therapy: Stoic Philosophy as Rational and Cognitive Psychotherapy*, Second Edition (London, New York: Routledge, 2020).

———. "Introduction to Stoicism: The Three Disciplines," February 20, 2013, https://donaldrobertson.name/2013/02/20/introduction-to-stoicism-the-three-disciplines/

———. "Stoic Philosophy as a Cognitive-Behavioral Therapy," *Medium*, September 15, 2019, originally published by D. Robertson and T. Codd in *The Behavior Therapist*, Vol. 42, No. 2, February 2019.

———. *How to Think Like a Roman Emperor: The Stoic Philosophy of Marcus Aurelius* (St. Martin's Press, New York: 2019).

Sadler, Gregory. "Self-Directed Study in Philosophy / Cicero's Philosophy / Sadler's advice, https://www.youtube.com/watch?v=Rts78oXDN_w&list=PL4gvlOxpKKIj tF5wHJy4xmlR2i8TgF59M.

———. "Is the Philosophy of Stoicism Self-Centered? Answers to Common Questions": https://www.youtube.com/watch?v=nuit5Kf5BH8.

———. "The Core Principles of Stoicism": https://www.youtube.com/watch?v=0IITtrea0sA.

———. "Philosophy Pop-Up with Dr. Sadler - September 2017 - Topic: Stoicism and 'In Accordance With Nature'": https://www.youtube.com/watch?v=4LTS21ZOtxE.

———. "Cicero, On the Nature of the Gods, book 2 - Introduction to Philosophy": https://www.youtube.com/watch?v=PVW3FD_Qxcg&list=PL4gvlOxpKKIjtF5w HJy4xmlR2i8TgF59M&index=5.

Sandburg, Carl. *Abraham Lincoln: The Prairie Years and the War Years* (New York: Harcourt, Brace and Company, 1926, 1939), One-Volume Edition.

Sellars, John. "Aligning with Your Nature, Finding Meaning & the Stoic Approach to Emotions": https://www.youtube.com/watch?v=dLZheK7ygIg.

———. How to Be a Stoic: Conversation with Donald J. Robertson: https://www.youtube.com/watch?v=ltFgRz-jhII.

Seneca, Lucius. *Letters from a Stoic*, adapted for the contemporary reader by James Harris, 2017.

———. *On Clemency* (Compass Circle, 2021).

Sensoy, Özlem, and Robin DiAngelo. *Is Everyone Really Equal? An Introduction to Key Concepts in Social Justice Education*, (New York: Teachers College Press, 2012).

Shenk, Joshua Wolf. *Lincoln's Melancholy* (New York: Houghton Mifflin Harcourt, 2005).

Smithsonian National Museum of African American History and Culture, "Whiteness: Talking about Race," https://nmaahc.si.edu/learn/talking-about-race/topics/whiteness.

St. George Stock. *A Guide to Stoicism* audiobook, https://www.youtube.com/watch?v=xlUE3WxZjiM.

Sugrue, Michael. Marcus Aurelius: Lecture on Stoicism: https://www.youtube.com/watch?v=L5_an6B3H4E.

Thrasher, Steven. "Claudia Rankine: Why I'm Spending $625,000 to Study Whiteness," *Guardian*, October 19, 2016.

Whiting, Kai, and Leonidas Konstantakos. *Being Better: Stoicism for a World Worth Living in* (Novato, CA: New World Library, 2021).

Wilson, Emily. *Seneca: A Life* (Penguin, 2016).

The Works of Abraham Lincoln, Vol. I, Abraham Lincoln: The True Story of a Great Life, Early Speeches 1832–1856 (New York: Newton & Cartwright; Current Literature Publishing Company, 1907).

The Works of Abraham Lincoln, Vol. II, Abraham Lincoln: Speeches and Debates, 1856–1859 (New York: Newton & Cartwright; Current Literature Publishing Company, 1907).

The Works of Abraham Lincoln, Vol. III, Abraham Lincoln: Speeches and Presidential Addresses, 1859–1865 (New York: Newton & Cartwright; Current Literature Publishing Company, 1907).

The Works of Abraham Lincoln, Vol. IV, Letters and Telegrams, Messages to Congress, Military Orders, Autobiography, Memoranda, Etc. (New York: Newton & Cartwright; Current Literature Publishing Company, 1907).

Index

critical race theory, 22, 47, 48, 60, 84, 86, 88, 97–98; interest convergence, 86; storytelling, 22
critical pedagogy, 47, 83
Critical Social Justice, xvii, xix–xxi, 2–4, 18–23, 25, 30, 32, 35, 45–46, 62, 73–77, 81, 83, 85–87, 89, 95, 97–99, 113, 130–131; consequentialist philosophy, 77
Critical Theory, xiii–xiv, xvi, 5, 20, 35, 47, 50, 59, 76–77, 81, 83–84, 86
critical whiteness studies, xxi, 86–90, 95
Cruise, Tom, 31–32
Crusoe, Robinson, 85
cult of ethnicity, 54
cultural appropriation, 51
cultural hegemony, 7
culture industry, 6, 9
cultural Marxism, 47
culture war, 47
Cynical Theories, 21, 47
cynics, 63–64
cynicism, 1, 66

Dakota War, 121–122
Davis, Angela, 47
"dead white males," 47, 54
de Botton, Alain, 72
Declaration of Independence, 119–121
Delgado, Richard, 22, 47; *Critical Race Theory: An Introduction* 22, 47; *Critical Race Theory: The Cutting Edge,* 22
Delphic oracle, 1, 63
Denby, David, 39, 54
Derrida, Jacques, 46, 48
Descartes, René, 68; clear and distinct ideas, 68
de-platform, 43
determinism, 30, 33, 65, 71
Dialectic of Enlightenment, 5–9, 17, 20
DiAngelo, Robin, xiii, xvi, xiv, 20, 47–49, 87–88, 91; white fragility, xiii–xiv, xxi, 88; *White Fragility: Why It's So Hard to Talk to White*

People about Racism, xiii, 87–88; *Is Everyone Really Equal? An Introduction to Key Concepts in Social Justice Education,* 20, 45
dichotomy of control, xxiv, xxv, xxvi, 18, 23, 34, 43, 63, 65, 70–73, 93, 130
Diogenes the Cynic, 77
disciplines, 61, 68–69; "exercise themes of Stoicism," 68; of desire, 61, 68–69; of action, 61, 68–69; of assent, 61, 68–69
discourse, xiv, xvi, 20–21, 28–29, 45, 48, 76, 83, 88, 94–97
Disney, 6
diversity, 28, 31–32, 87, 89, 91; training; 28, 87
Douglas, Stephen, 115, 118–121
Douglass, Frederick, 87, 109, 112, 115, 117, 119, 122; *Narrative of the Life of Frederick Douglass*, 87
Dred Scott decision, 109
Drew, Simon, 106
Drug Enforcement Agency, 99
Drusus, 71
DuBois, W. E. B., 86

Eclipse of Reason, 20
economics, 9–12, 18; cost-benefit analysis, 9, 18; identity economics 9
efficiency, 9–12, 14–15, 17–18
elements, 67; air, 67; earth, 67; fire, 67; water, 67
Emancipation Proclamation, 112–113, 115, 121, 123
Empiricism, 21, 67
Emory University, 46; Black Students at Emory University, 46
emotion(s) xiii, 24–25, 34, 41, 66, 71, 74, 99–100, 131
"end of history," 48–49
Enlightenment, xiii, 5, 7–9, 21–22, 30
Epaphroditus, 70–72, 73
Epictetus, 18, 23, 32, 40, 44, 65, 68–75, 85, 92, 108, 113, 118, 129–130; *Discourses*, 23, 32–33,

About the Author

Jonathan D. Church is an economist with two decades of experience working in the private and public sectors. His professional background is in antitrust, intellectual property, valuation, inflation, index number theory, statistics, and finance. In 2016, he began writing a weekly column for *The Good Men Project*, with a focus on current affairs, social justice, and masculinity. Outside of his day job and time with his daughter, he spends most of his remaining time as an independent scholar writing on economics, finance, philosophy, and cultural issues. He has been published in *Quillette*, *Areo*, *Arc Digital*, *The Agonist Journal*, *Merion West*, the Good Men Project, *Culturico, New Discourses, The Washington Examiner, The Daily Stoic*, and *The Federalist*. He has also published poetry in *Lummox, Big Hammer*, and *Street Value*, as well as short stories in *Vending Machine Press* and *The Agonist Journal*. His book, *Reinventing Racism: Why 'White Fragility' Is the Wrong Way to Think about Racial Inequality*, was published by Rowman & Littlefield in December 2020. He graduated from the University of Pennsylvania with a BA in economics and philosophy, and from Cornell University with an MA in economics. He is also a CFA charter holder.

www.ingramcontent.com/pod-product-compliance
Lightning Source LLC
Chambersburg PA
CBHW030652270326
41929CB00007B/331